Compact Library Shelving

L T P PUBLICATIONS · NO. 14

Compact Library Shelving

by Drahoslav Gawrecki

Translated from the Czech
by Stanislav Rehak

LIBRARY TECHNOLOGY PROGRAM

AMERICAN LIBRARY ASSOCIATION

Chicago

Originally published in Czechoslovakia as: *Nové regálové zařízení v zahraničních knihovnách (New Shelving Equipment in Libraries Abroad)*, Martin: Matica Slovenská, 1960

Foreword

In 1964, I agreed to review the literature relating to compact book storage for a special issue of *Library Trends*[1] devoted to library furniture and furnishings. In this connection I encountered some documentation that was unintelligble to me because it was written in languages with which I was not familiar, and for which it was difficult to find competent translators. Fortunately, I succeeded in obtaining a small grant for translation services from the Library Technology Project (now the Library Technology Program) of the American Library Association, through the interest of its former Director, Frazer G. Poole. The translations that resulted were made by non-library language experts and were in no sense intended for publication; their purpose was merely to give me a rough impression of the content, so that I could more meaningfully allude to the publications than by merely listing them as bibliographic references. The items under consideration were a book by a Czechoslovakian author, Drahoslav Gawrecki, and two articles from Eastern Eurpean library journals. After having perused the translations, I was convinced that Gawrecki had made a most comprehensive and penetrating study of compact storage ideas. Concerning the other two authors, I thought that they had presented competent reviews and evaluations of some of the more pertinent literature and of the compact storage installations they knew about. I was impressed by the knowledgeability, the reasoning skill, and the thoroughness of all three authors; I also admired their enterprise in including in their appraisal foreign installations, many of which they had not been able to inspect but had merely read about.

Subsequently, Mr. Forrest F. Carhart, Jr., the present Director of the Library Technology Program, proposed the idea of having the Gawrecki translation edited and published, together with some material selected from Gawrecki's bibliography, in order to

---

1. "Economics of Compact Book Shelving," *Library Trends*, XIII (April, 1965), 433-47.

provide some basic information and to stimulate thinking on an important technological topic that has so far received only sporadic attention and about which there has been relatively little theoretical research in the U.S.

Compact storage of books has not been a central concern among library managers in the U.S., partly because American libraries have tended, or preferred, to provide open and ready access even to little-used books (and compact shelving would presumably have made them less accessible), partly because libraries have rarely segregated more frequently from less frequently used books on a systematic basis. Other reasons are that American librarians have not become fully convinced that compact storage has sufficient advantages to offset its obvious disadvantages as long as land and building funds continue to be relatively plentiful, and the commercially available equipment relatively high in price and hard to write specifications for in situations that require competitive bidding. Moreover, the choice of readily procurable equipment has been limited, there are relatively few manufacturers that have done much to promote the sale of compact storage equipment, and some manufacturers have even discontinued their product lines, evidently for lack of sustained demand. Other manufacturers have continued to offer the drawer-type of compact shelving but probably have not sold a great deal compared to conventional stacks. One American firm, Jackson Compactus, some years ago reported that it had acquired the franchise for the Compactus undercarriage design developed by the Swiss inventor, Hans Ingold, but no large Compactus library installation was apparently contracted for or built for an American library. Jackson Compactus later discontinued manufacturing the Ingold products, changed its name to Jackson Storage Systems, and developed its own line of equipment. We understand, however, that it recently went out of business altogether. A similar design of electrically or manually movable stack blocks (Elecompack) had been shown at the New York ALA Conference in 1965, but has so far apparently found no takers for its franchise among American manufacturers. However, an important factor in the low interest shown by American librarians in compact shelving has probably been a lack of informed discussion on the subject.

The problems of optimal space utilization and economical book storage, especially for little-used books, continue to be critical in libraries everywhere. Large university and research libraries continually have to grapple with space problems, and if their present rate of growth continues, the pressures will become ever more intense as available space and shelves become filled and land areas around library buildings become increasingly scarce or exorbitantly expensive. However, manufacturers are not likely to develop a multitude of reasonably-priced competitive designs until they can detect and project a market for such products. To what extent compact storage represents a solution to the book congestion problem of libraries is still an open question, but it is one that certainly deserves more attention than it has received thus far.

The contributions presented in this volume are not intended to form a comprehensive and definitive treatment of the subject, but rather to serve as a departure for further deliberation, exploration, and experimentation by library practitioners, engineers, and equipment manufacturers. The purpose of the volume is not to promote the idea of compact book storage as such, but rather to stimulate thinking as to justifiable applications, available alternatives, and the theory behind it.

Gawrecki's contribution is particularly notable in the area of theory of stack-space utilization. What kinds of arrangements are conceivable? What combinations of different types of equipment are most advantageous? He makes the point that we cannot glibly talk about percentage increases in capacity offered by different types of equipment without first making certain that the area available for book storage is suitably designed (with regard to dimension, obstructions, etc.) for a particular type of equipment, and that what is most suitable for one type of equipment is most likely much less suitable for a different type of equipment or different combinations of equipment. In his treatment, he is primarily concerned about space utilization rather than overall financial advantages. In spite of the fact that Gawrecki's work was originally published some years ago, it still remains one of the most thorough discussions of the theoretical aspects of compact shelving available today.

It was originally intended to publish only the Gawrecki book in this volume. However, as a convenience to the reader, the Library Technology Program has, rightly I think, decided to include some of the more important material from the author's bibliography. The items were chosen either because it was felt that they would add significantly to the information contained in Gawrecki's work, or that they would represent certain points of view on compact shelving which would be of special interest to the reader.

Because this volume is basically intended to present a translation of Gawrecki's work and selected items from his bibliography, no attempt has been made to bring the material up to date by including articles published after the original Czech publication of Gawrecki's book. Consequently, some of the material in this volume is now obsolete in the sense that some of the equipment described is no longer manufactured, or has since been modified or manufactured in a different form, and some of the manufacturers mentioned are no longer active in the compact shelving field. The basic theories and ideas presented are, however, still valid, and should, as was said before, serve as a basis for further probing into a subject which may, in the future, assume much more importance in library technology than it has in the past.

Drahoslav Gawrecki, the principal contributor to this volume, was visited in Prague by Mr. Carhart in September, 1966. Mr. Carhart found Gawrecki most cooperative and friendly, and very much interested in having an English translation of his work published in the United States. He generously agreed to supply originals of illustrations and clarifications of his text to make the translation as accurate as possible.

Gawrecki is considered a recognized authority in matters relating to library layout, furniture, and equipment in Eastern Europe. He has assembled in his office in the State Library of the Czechoslovak Socialist Republic, where he has been working as Head of the Technical Department, a comprehensive file of information on library equipment, perhaps the most comprehensive in Eastern Europe. Mr. Gawrecki, who was born in 1919, has authored over 350 articles and publications, and has served as Director of two city libraries, a scientific library, and a university library, and as a provincial library inspector. His influence extends far beyond the boundaries of his small country into other Socialist republics. He is known for his ability to delve deeply into important topics often neglected by others in the field of library planning and library equipment. In his present position, he is concerned with library mechanization, the planning of a new building for the Central Czechoslovak Library, library building preservation and restoration, photoreproduction, and technical library equipment generally.

In addition to providing basic information on compact shelving, and its value as a stimulation of further thinking on a somewhat neglected subject, this present volume will serve, I hope, as still another proof, if any is needed, that the same problems, and an active interest in finding common solutions to them, are to be found everywhere in the world today among professional librarians, regardless of the political or economic systems in which the library as an institution happens to exist.

> Robert H. Muller
> *Associate Director*
> *The University of Michigan Library*
> *Ann Arbor, Michigan*

The original Czechoslovak edition of Gawrecki's work appeared in five parts in three separately published volumes. Volume 1 contained Parts One and Two, Volume 2 contained Part Three, and Volume 3 contained Parts Four and Five.

Because of this form of publication, there is a certain amount of repetition in some sections of the book.

We have preserved the footnote arrangement of the original publication, there being a separate set of notes for each of the original volumes. We have, however, omitted the partial bibliographies which were originally printed in Volumes 2 and 3, and have placed the complete bibliography—to which we have added our own brief annotations—at the end of Part Five.

Gawrecki's work as it appears here is almost entirely a direct translation of the original. Neither the author nor the editor has attempted to revise (with one exception, noted in the text), or to update the material. Consequently, as Mr. Muller noted in his Foreword, some of the specific types of equipment described are either no longer manufactured, or are being manufactured under different trade names.

The Library Technology Program hopes that the publication of this book will stimulate further research on compact shelving and that it will be possible to publish information in the near future on the newer compact shelving equipment.

We had hoped to reproduce all of Gawrecki's original illustrations. However, due to the lapse of time between the Czech publication and the present one, we were not able to obtain all of the original artwork. We have made substitutions for a few of the original photographs, and some of the drawings have been slightly revised by the author for this volume.

We are unable to obtain most of the illustrations for the article by F. N. Pashchenko in Appendix A. In many instances, however, the illustrations used in the original Gawrecki and Pashchenko texts were identical. Consequently, we have referred the reader to the pertinent illustrations in the Gawrecki text whenever we felt this to be necessary or helpful. We were also unable to obtain the illustrations that originally appeared in the articles by Kromnow and Tell (Appendices B, C, and D). However, these illustrations were very few in number, and largely repetitious of those appearing elsewhere in this volume.

The articles by Hill (Appendix E) and Muller (Appendix F) are, for all practical purposes, exact reprints of the originals, and no attempt was made to edit them for this publication.

Most of the non-English materials listed in the Gawrecki bibliography have been translated and are on file in the office of the Library Technology Program at ALA headquarters in Chicago.

Herbert L. Hanna
Library Technology Program

Contents

Author's Preface

Libraries, archives, and various other establishments abroad are using several types of new shelving equipment to increase the storage capacity for their collections.

It is commonly recognized that storage space is used with relative inefficiency when shelving equipment of the traditional type, such as that widely used in Czechoslovakia, is employed. On the average, this type of shelving utilizes only 30 to 35 percent of the floor space in the standard arrangement of a storage facility. This 1:2 ratio of the floor area used for ranges to that used for aisles can be substantially improved by employing new types of shelving, and more suitable conditions for the effective use of library space can also be obtained in this manner.

This possibility, which has been proved repeatedly in practice abroad, has caused our librarians to demand the introduction of new, but proven shelving equipment into our libraries and archives.

We have as yet had no practical experience with the new equipment. However, on the basis of literature and incomplete reports from foreign sources we have formed a general image of the new shelving techniques. We are convinced that the new equipment will help our libraries to reduce the problems resulting from collections which are now often unsuitably placed and insufficiently protected, and which are consequently inefficiently organized, easily damaged, and difficult to use, especially when we consider the fact that collections are now often rapidly outgrowing currently available storage space.

While our librarians do not oversimplify the problem of the placement, protection, and use of collections, they do see that a substantial portion of their difficulties can be attributed to obsolete storage equipment. I have had the opportunity in lectures, discussions, and workshops to focus attention on the solutions to this problem which have been achieved in the Soviet Union, the United States, Britain, Sweden, Switzerland, Canada, Germany, France, and elsewhere. As access to foreign literature in this field is limited and often insufficient, and personal answers to individual questions are not always possible, our librarians have asked for more easily available information in printed form. The use of new storage equipment is not limited to libraries; there are also commercial and industrial applications, all of which involve planners, construction engineers, technicians, and research institutes as well as manufacturers. All the people involved need to study the principles of compact storage equipment and compact storage buildings, as well as the construction and properties of existing equipment and its applications. As the author of several contributions in the field of compact storage and the organization of warehousing space, I have received requests from many persons for information, materials, documentation, and proposals on compact shelving suitable for use in Czechoslovakia.

In 1958 I announced the forthcoming publication of a study entitled "Economical Organization of the Storage, Protection, and Use of Collections in Libraries" ("Ekonomická organisace umístění, ochrany a používání fondů v knihovnách"), which would be more thorough and complete than any existing work in this field available abroad, but for various reasons the manuscript has not yet been published [still unpublished as this book goes to press]. The present work is intended to give at least brief descriptions and illustrations of the products available abroad and a list of the most important literature.

I do not consider this present short work as a definitive one. It can serve to give some preliminary information, but it cannot constitute a complete evaluation of the purpose, usefulness, and actual value of compact shelf equipment because such equipment cannot be objectively evaluated without an analysis of the whole complex of problems connected with the storage, protection, and use of collections in libraries and archives, and without an expert and careful study of each individual case.

The new types of storage equipment are understandably more demanding in terms of construction than the standard cases still exclusively used in our country; the properties of this equipment which make possible better employment of available storage space also pose special technical and organizational problems. However, when we consider the evolutionary changes through which libraries had to pass before they achieved the now traditional storage racks, we should not be deterred by the prospect that each increase in effectiveness will require new and often radical modifications, especially now when sufficient improvement can no longer be obtained by a simple reorganization of existing storage facilities, but must utilize new technology to be really effective.

The theory of the organization of storage space is not yet sufficiently developed, and libraries are not always prepared to make the most effective installations of this type of equipment, either in terms of building construction or of technical knowledge.

It would therefore be possible for some libraries to obtain far less effective results than could be achieved in theory even though costly new installations of equipment were to be made.

It is therefore necessary to study the whole complex problem of shelving and the use of storage space thoroughly and to give careful attention to all its phases.

May I recommend that interested individuals direct their questions to the Chair of Library Science in Prague, where Dr. Jaroslav Drtina and Dr. Jiří Kábrt specialize in the new technical arrangements for libraries, or to Dr. J. Těšitel in the Library of the University of Chemical Technology in Pardubice. I will gladly contribute the data and literature that I have available. From my personal experience I also have no doubt that our Soviet friends, the architects F. N. Pashchenko, G. V. Meyendorf, and the engineer A. S. Sabitov in Moscow, and A. A. Songina and V. A. Marin in Leningrad will readily answer questions and supply information upon request.

I should like to take this opportunity to express my sincere thanks to these Soviet friends as well as to Director W. Piasecki, J. Bleton, Dr. R. Stromeyer, Hans Ingold, Robert H. Muller, and to various foreign manufacturers for the information and literature made available to me. I am also much obliged to Director R. Pittermann, Dr. J. Těšitel, M. Novotná, A. Řihová, O. Lányová, and M. Tvardková for their help in the collection and evaluation of the material and to Director J. Paška and the co-workers of Matica Slovenská for the speedy publication of my manuscript.

PART ONE

General Characteristics
of Compact Shelves

I   Compact shelves are a special type of storage
equipment which makes possible a substantial increase in the capacity of storage space through various arrangements of units, sections, and complete shelving systems, as well as by an adaptation
of the shelf loading surfaces themselves. The construction, organization, and method of employment of this equipment differ
in a larger or smaller degree from the traditional cases and
traditional storage equipment of all types.

The storage of collections shelved with this equipment is
known as "compact storage" because of the higher degree of
compactness achieved. (In Czech, it is known as "skladování
kompaktní"; in Russian [transliterated], "kompaktnoje knigo-
chranenie"; in French, "magasinage dense"; in German, "kompact-
magazinierung"; in Polish, "magazynowanie zwarte"; in Italian,
"scaffalature compatta"; etc.).

Storage space arranged by the use of this equipment is
called "compact storage space," although in speaking of compact
storage space we think above all about its architectural solution
and the design which will ensure conditions necessary for achieving maximum capacity and the best utilization of the space. However, correctly used, compact equipment, whether alone or in
conjunction with additional standard cases of traditional types,
will impart the characteristics of compact storage space even
to an area which was not designed for it. This may require special
adaptations, depending on the construction characteristics of the
building in which it is being installed.

Compact storage sections are either complementary or inde-
dependent.[1] By complementary compact sections we mean the
equipment used to complement the basic units of the stationary
cases, ranges, and systems used in ordinary or conventional
storage practice. In their original form, these sections were

characteristically used as additions to an existing system of stationary cases. They were added to these systems as either mechanically joined structural parts or loosely added independent structures, and were placed in the spaces which were not utilized by the original equipment, but which were devoted to communications and staff work operations. In newer constructions, some types of complementary shelving developed into compact equipment which could be used independently from the traditional stationary cases and placed in a separate part of the installation. By independent compact sections, therefore, we mean basic units which can be used independently from any other equipment, whether as separate individual installations, or used in various combinations with systems made up of different types of units.

II   A compactly organized storage space can be equipped with:

(a) independent compact sections in a single system using one or more makes of units;

(b) combined systems of independent compact sections in several different systems using one or more makes of units;

(c) combined systems of independent compact sections and complementary compact sections in one or more systems using one or more makes of units;

(d) combined systems of independent compact sections in one or more systems using one or more makes of units and stationary shelves of the traditional type;

(e) combined systems of stationary shelves of the traditional type and complementary compact sections in one or more systems using one or more makes of units;

(f) combined systems of stationary shelves of the traditional type, independent compact sections, and complementary compact sections, where the compact sections may be in one or more systems using one or more makes of units.

Equipment used in a particular storage place can be considered either as the basic installation or as a supplementary installation depending on the number of units, sections, and combinations, and on their function. The basic installation is the one that is used in the main storage area and fills the largest proportion of the area.

Within this meaning even the independent sections may be considered a supplementary installation.

Compact shelving used abroad at the present time falls basically into the following types:

(1) stationary shelves combined with movable revolving segments

(2) stationary shelves with movable drawers

(3) movable sliding shelves.[2]

Each of these types of compact shelves is produced at the present time in several structural variations and makes.

All *revolving* compact shelves use a suspended construction with vertically hung hinged sections of various types, possibly combined with a guide rail arrangement.

Several types of revolving shelf sections are produced; they do not vary much in principle, but there is a difference in their effectiveness, mainly in relation to the size of the area necessary for aisles. The total degree of compactness is not very high. The cost of the fixtures themselves is reasonable, but there is a general increase in building costs for some types of these fixtures. Their use is limited in many cases to new buildings designed specifically for their use, or to basement floor space which can bear the increased load. Their use has been limited since 1950 to the United States and France, where these products are installed under a licensing arrangement. The independently movable individual loading surfaces (shelves) suggested by F. Rider have not yet found a practical application. [Fremont Rider, *Compact Book Storage*, New York: Hadham Press, 1949, p. 32.]

In Czechoslovakia, it is probable that we could achieve a certain amount of improvement in this type of equipment by modifying the design. All the theoretical possibilities, such as a system of both single- and double-wing units and their various combinations, have not yet been fully achieved in practice. In many instances a combined system, using the revolving type together with sliding shelves, should be considered.

The stationary shelf sections with movable drawer-like shelves, the so-called *drawer-type* compact cases, are constructed in a manner similar to vertical file drawers and are equipped with ball-bearing rollers. The currently most widely used drawer-type cases are relatively well made from a technical point of view, but they are substantially more complex and thus place more critical demands on manufacture than other compact systems. These cases are used to any great extent at the present time only in the United States, although some are being used experimentally in the Soviet Union, but they can possibly also be used here to advantage, mainly in specialized conditions. The consensus seems to be, however, that they are not one of the most effective types of compact shelving.

In our opinion, the applicability of drawer-type shelving will have to be re-evaluated when it is considered as being used in combination with movable sliding shelves, especially those which slide sideways; and we expect that this combined type of system will provide an important contribution to the economic organization of space with maximum effectiveness. For this reason, we cannot, at the present time, accept without reservation the unfavorable evaluation of drawer-type equipment which is often found in professional circles in Europe today.

On the basis of experience with existing foreign drawer-type products already in use we can expect only minor improvements when their production starts in our country, mostly in the direction of simplified frame construction and the modification of shelf drawers to correspond to our own requirements.

Movable *sliding shelves* may use either hangers or undercarriages. The hanger type is normally constructed with top rail tracks, while the undercarriage type is constructed with wheels or rollers, having either a free movement, or a movement on rails fixed in the floor.

These shelf units may be classified by the direction of their movement into sideways or laterally moving [moving parallel to their length—i.e., "parallel sliding"], and frontally moving [perpendicular to their length—i.e., "perpendicular sliding"]. Their advantage lies in simple construction; there is, however, one disadvantage inherent in some of those which use rails. This disadvantage results from the necessary special preparation of the floor space, which, in turn, sometimes results in an installation of a permanent character, and consequently in increased costs. Sliding compact shelves are generally very effective; parallel sliding shelves are demonstrably the most effective among all the types of compact equipment used at the present time. Even in their present state of development they are several times more effective than stationary cases. At the same time, their construction is uncomplicated, and their use is simple. They are now being used in a number of countries because of these advantages. Libraries, archives, and other establishments in the Soviet Union plan to use them for storage requirements, both in old buildings and in new projects. They are being manufactured in the United States, Britain, Sweden, Switzerland, East

Germany, and France, and are being used in other countries as well (for example, in Canada and Finland). In other countries, such as Italy and Poland, they are currently a subject of research or of practical testing, as in Austria.

The newest Soviet research and planning show, however, that all the advantages of sliding shelves, both in construction and organization, have not yet been fully realized. The direction of development indicates quite persuasively that significant improvements are possible. There is no doubt that the most effective systems achieved in the future will be formed with the use of sliding shelves.

Revolving and drawer-type shelves are moved by hand. Sliding shelves can be moved by hand or can be fully or semi-automatic. Electric motors or pneumatic systems are used as a power source.

Metals are most often used in the production of the equipment; however, some wood, plastics, and synthetic materials of various types are also used.

The degree of compactness varies, as can be observed even from this brief description of the general characteristics of the main types of equipment. This degree of compactness depends not only on the basic characteristics of the individual shelving units, sections, and systems, and on the properties which can be obtained by combining various types, but also on other conditions, which may be specific for each library, archive, or other type of installation.

Suitable application in terms of overall effectiveness cannot, then, be fully evaluated in general terms; the solution of each storage problem must be considered individually, according to the type of the establishment involved, the type and function of the collections, and prevailing technical conditions.

The three general types of compact shelves described above do not represent a complete list of available equipment; but other types mentioned by various authors are not important in practice at the present time. We have insufficient information about some types—for example, the compact type "four-way bookstacks"—which are undoubtedly interesting both in their structure and use.[3] Others merely represent early stage proposals, and not fully realized ideas or executed plans. The conceptions of F. Rider[4] and the proposal of H. Aumund[5] can serve as extreme examples of this type of plan.

Compact shelving represents a tremendous and not yet fully appreciated advance in library technology. However, it is wrong to state that its introduction and its further technical improvement will solve, by itself, the problems of storage space (a statement often made not only in manufacturers' literature, but also by librarians and other specialists). Without doubt, the future belongs to compact shelving, but not as the sole or final solution.

Although we evaluate compact shelving in a positive manner and do not accept the negative stand of its opponents, who are often perhaps too conservative and who are also sometimes unduly influenced by individual circumstances which may make practical introduction of the new techniques difficult, it is our opinion that all arguments and all factors must be subjected to critical evaluation, to serious analysis, and to comprehensive research, and that it would be incorrect to be satisfied with the results which have been obtained up to the present time. A large amount of creative work is waiting for the proponents of compact shelving, and for all of us who daily work as research workers, engineers, or technicians in the field of library and storage technology. We must all try to contribute to better use of the new techniques if we are to help make full use of all the undeniable advantages of these installations and at the same time reduce to a minimum some of their inherent disadvantages.

PART TWO

Revolving Compact Shelves

I   Modern revolving compact shelves belong to a type of storage equipment which is based on the application of a principle which was already known when stationary cases were almost exclusively used, and even before the stationary shelves now known as the traditional type became standardized. The current products are only variations of the original individual "prototypes" which have been improved by new production techniques. They cannot be considered purely the result of the theory of compact storage in the sense in which this theory is known and applied at present. They are in fact the result of the empirical trial-and-error methods of the past which usually resulted in only minor improvements, although in a few instances, it must be admitted, with results that we have not been able to equal even today. They constitute only one of the methods which have been used to solve the problem of how to utilize excess aisle space for storage purposes.

The storage in many libraries is still organized in such a way that the distance between centers of stationary shelf ranges frequently exceeds, for one reason or another, the standard dimension [125 cm.]; such distance is excessive and serves no purpose.

When we consider that this center-to-center distance ranges from 480 cm. (at Göttingen for example) to an average of 300 to 320 cm. (Bibliothèque Nationale, Paris), or 200 to 210 cm. (Basel, Marburg, Wolfenbüttel), or 150 cm. (Cracow [1930], Bern [1931], Grenoble [1955], Ghent [1938], Darmstadt [1954], etc.), it is clear that there exist considerable reserves which would make substantial increases in storage capacity possible. This is evident even in new buildings.

Librarians who in the past have faced the difficult problem of insufficient space for new acquisitions have always searched for new and more effective solutions. They did not all proceed in the same way and thus have left for us a fund of worthwhile experience as a result of the various methods they used. Some of these past methods will be more fully described when we deal with the individual systems of compact shelves with which these methods are connected.

At this time, however, it seems useful to mention the experiment of the English librarian, Charles G. Virgo, who in the years 1878 to 1884 in the Bradford Free Library used a design (described by F. J. Hill[6] and F. N. Pashchenko[7]), considered to be the most original solution of this type. In this installation, a movable hinged case was fastened to the stationary cabinet bookcase. The books placed in the inside layer, i.e., the books on the shelves of the original stationary case, were accessible in the new arrangement only when the hinged case was turned open in a movement similar to the opening of a door. The stability of the movable hinged case was increased by a roller fastened to the outside edge, which moved in a metal groove. Cases of this type were used in the Bradford Free Library until the year 1903. There are no existing reports about the use of this particular equipment in other libraries, and F. J. Hill assumes from this that the installation was not an unqualified success. He expresses the opinion that it was the wooden construction which was probably the main cause of its imperfections. The fact that American manufacturers use an identical principle for their products, for which, however, they use metal or other non-wood material, seems to attest to the correctness of this opinion.

The addition of one hinged movable case will create out of an original single-faced stationary case either a double-layered or a triple-layered revolving compact case, depending on whether the added hinged case is single- or double-faced. The hinging of two revolving cases, one on either side of an original double-faced stationary case, will create either a four-layered or six-layered revolving compact bookcase, again depending upon the construction of the hinged case.

Bookcases of this type are generally called "single-turn" or "single-wing" cases because of the fact that the hinged case is of one-piece design and swings open as a single unit.

The revolving cases proper, i.e., the movable segments which make the formation of this type of compact bookcase possible, are most typically used as complementary shelves. Revolving segments without a central stationary loading surface do not exist as independent installations.

II   The ideas which led to the creation of the first revolving bookcases also imprinted the principal typical features on present-day products. Structural improvements and the perfection of the techniques of manufacture are, after all, essentially only added refinements. The original overall design has not been changed in any basic way. We can summarize, therefore, that all the modern products of revolving cases are substantially identical with the original revolving-case adaptations of the traditional stationary bookcase.

The stationary, single- or double-faced bookcase remains as the basic unit of revolving compact shelving of all types.

In a unit with one hinged movable case, the stationary case is located in the rear part of the compact unit; in a unit with two hinged movable cases, it is located in the center.

The revolving segments are sometimes loosely added to the stationary case, but more often they are connected directly by lateral suspension. In a loosely added arrangement the suspended structure is usually installed on a separate load-bearing upright; in a solid connection the revolving segments are connected directly to the frame structure of the stationary case. The vertical axis, or hinge, around which the revolving segment makes its circular movement, may be located either on the outside or on the inside of the left or right end of the revolving case. [See for example, drawings I and II, Fig. 1.] The revolving movement, which is actuated by hand, resembles the opening and closing of doors or casement windows. The effect is in fact somewhat different, however, because the revolving segments have a much more substantial thickness. When the axis is located on the outer side of the revolving segment, the entire end panel of the movable portion of the arrangement remains in the aisle in front of the stationary case when opened 90°; its position parallel with the end panel of the stationary section is reached only when opened 180°, when the movable section moves into the space in front of the neighboring case (or in the space of the adjoining side passage). When opened 90° or less, the entire movable section is in the aisle in front of the stationary section; it moves into the space in front of the adjoining unit (or the area of adjoining side passage) only when it is opened more than 90°. When the axis is located on the inside of the revolving segment, the end panel of the movable part of the arrangement passes into the space in front of the neighboring case or the adjoining side passage immediately upon being opened to any degree. Consequently, the latter type has only a limited application.

The amount of aisle space required for revolving segments depends on their design and on their dimensions, as will be noted later on. It should be remembered that the method of passing into the spaces of the aisles in front of the neighboring cases or into the areas of adjacent side passages is important for the degree of compactness and the attainable capacity of the storage area.

The area required for the revolving movement depends on the angle required for opening the unit completely; this angle is at least 90°, but more often 110° to 120°, and in some designs 180°. It was already mentioned that the revolving segment describes a circular path (a quarter-circle, or a half-circle) around a stationary axis. The length of the area required for the movement is equal to the length of the diagonal of the rectangular area of the revolving segment of the section.

When the revolving segment of an opened case is located in either the front aisle or in the side aisle, the width required for those aisles depends on the dimensions of the revolving segments. In front aisles, it must always be equal to or greater than the length of the diagonal of the rectangular area of the revolving segment. [In the side passage, it is, of course, equal to or greater than the straight length of the segment.]

It follows then that the standardized width of aisles cannot be maintained when equipment containing revolving segments of a length similar to that of standard stationary sections 1 meter (39.37 inches) in length is used.

Since each widening of aisles above the minimum acceptable dimension (which is determined by safety regulations and work needs) decreases the actual capacity of the storage place, some revolving compact cases are produced with deliberately shortened revolving segments. These are the so-called double-turn or double-wing revolving bookcases. The revolving segments in a double-wing case are divided into two sections, half (or less) the length of the stationary case, and which swing open independently.

The suspension is located either at the center of the stationary case, or at each side.

The collections placed in the stationary case are inaccessible in the basic (closed) position of the unit. Similarly, collections placed on the inside of the revolving segments, when such segments are double-faced, are not accessible when the case is closed. Only the collections located in the front face of the revolving segments are freely accessible in this position.

14

A compact unit with a single-face stationary case may exist with two or three layers (or faces) according to the type of the revolving segment. This is evident from the diagrammatic plans of the principal systems of revolving compact shelves [Fig. 1]

Fig. 1   *Principal systems of revolving shelves.*

[The following group of drawings is collectively referred to as Fig. 1, with the individual drawings labeled "I" through "X". The letters within the drawings, designating the component parts, stand for the following—Editor]:

R — *Length of stationary case.*

0 — *Length of revolving segment.*

P — *Difference in length between the revolving segment and the stationary case.*

S — *Hinge point, or axis, about which the revolving segment turns.*

ₚ — *Width of area required for revolving segment in open position.*

P_p — *Total area required for revolving segment in open position.*

ᵣ — *Length of turning path of revolving segment.*

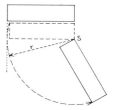

I

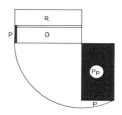

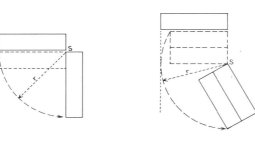

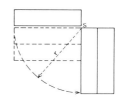

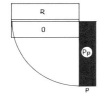

II

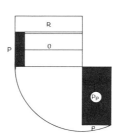

III

IV

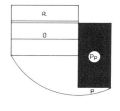

and from our description of the installation used by Charles G. Virgo in the Bradford Free Library. A compact unit with a double-face stationary case may have four or six layers, again

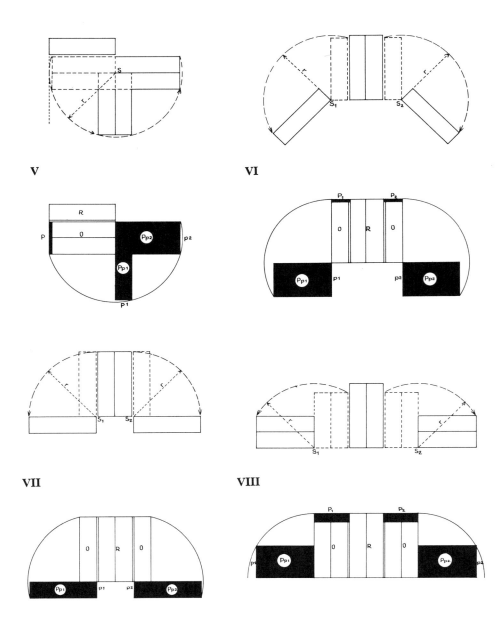

V   VI

VII   VIII

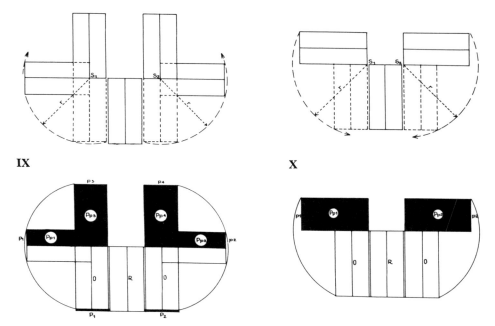

IX   X

depending on the type of the revolving segments, i.e., whether
they are single- or double-faced.

The following rule covers the amount of direct or indirect
access to the collections: in a single-faced revolving case in basic
(closed) position only one-half (in a two-layer case), or one-
third (in a three-layer case) of the collection is accessible in this
position.

The question of direct or indirect accessibility of the stored
collections is repeatedly emphasized because indirect access is a
typical characteristic of compact shelving, and in some systems
even results in the complete elimination of direct access to the
collection.

This indirect access to a part or to all of the stored collections
is an inescapable disadvantage of compact storage shelves of
every type produced up to now. It complicates working procedures and also requires a more complex technique for the
selection and filing of collections. It also increases the time required for these operations and to some extent reduces the advantages of shortened communications which are a positive feature of compact storage installations. Thus against the advantages

of the reduced ratio of aisle area to storage area and shortened communications must be weighed the disadvantage of more costly operating procedures.[8]

There is one more property peculiar to the revolving type of compact equipment which is a disadvantage, and that is that the depth of the side walls or end panels of the revolving segments limits the revolving segments to total lengths shorter than that of the stationary case. This of course decreases the total storage area on the shelves of the revolving segments and consequently the useful capacity of the complete structure. The advantage of the increased degree of compactness is thus in practice always reduced by a certain percentage.

One problem in the technical design of the revolving movement is solved in some structures by wheeled undercarriages fastened to the revolving segments, which move on rails or in a groove cut into the floor. This method lightens the load on the suspension system and increases the stability of the entire structure.

In the placement of the revolving cases, and therefore in the consideration of the basic organization of a storage area equipped with these cases, it is important to remember that a single-faced unit can either be placed along a wall or coupled with another unit. In coupling, two single-faced units are placed together back to back. This, in effect, creates a combination similar to a double-faced unit. Coupled, single-faced units have the same properties as double-faced units. They cannot be placed next to a wall because their revolving segments must be free to move out in the direction of the aisles.

III   Revolving compact shelves were until recently used only in the United States, but in the last few years they have been introduced into France.

They have been installed in several American university and public libraries, as well as in other archives and administrative locations. According to R. Stromeyer, writing in 1958, two archives and a scientific establishment in France had been equipped with this type of installation.[9]

We are familiar with the products known as the "Com-Pac-Case Storage System," produced by Art Metal Inc., and the "Compact Snead System," supplied by Snead & Company, which is represented in France by Les Forges de Strasbourg ("Snead-Strafor").

The best detailed data at our disposal concern the installation which was produced by Snead & Company specifically for the Midwest Inter-Library Center (MILC) [now the Center for Research Libraries] in Chicago in 1951.[10] This system was created through the collaboration of the architectural firm of Shaw, Metz, and Dolio and Ralph T. Esterquest, at that time director of the center which had been formed to serve as a depository library for a number of American university libraries. They studied various systems of compact shelves used at the time in Britain, Canada, and the United States. It is open to question whether they knew about the sliding cases of the "Compactus-Ingold" type, which had been granted a patent in 1947, but which were not produced in England until later.

The special structure and dimensions of the MILC installation were influenced to a considerable degree by the individual needs of that library, but we are going to give a short description of it here, not only because this particular installation has attracted much attention, but also because it has been used in foreign literature as a basis for comparisons between the systems of compact revolving shelves and compact sliding shelves.[11]

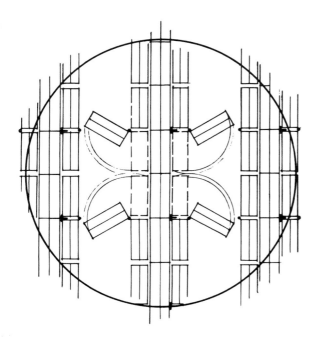

Fig. 2

Floor plan detail of MILC.

Fig. 3   *Revolving compact cases in MILC.*

A proper evaluation of a revolving compact shelf system cannot be made solely on the basis of this installation, or only on the basis of other equipment made by Snead & Company or the existing products of Art Metal Inc.[12] In our opinion it is necessary to investigate all the possibilities of a system of revolving shelves and then to determine the possibilities which could be expected from more efficient future types of this equipment. Though there are presently a relatively large number of rather serious disadvantages in the use of revolving shelves, we should not be satisfied with the unfavorable evaluations which are too often accepted today without question or objective proof.[13]

IV   The compact rotating shelving installed in the Midwest Inter-Library Center in 1951 has a load-bearing construction which is part of the structure of the building. The main load-bearing columns pass through all the floors of the building. The construction module is based on column-spacing intervals of 222 by 182 cm. The central part of the installation—the interior double-faced stationary cases—is connected to the load-bearing structure through the connection of two units to each load-bearing column. Directly on each column, above and below the ceiling, is the bearing shoulder, which supports a concrete ceiling 15 cm. thick. The shoulder at the same time provides support for steel girders for the installation of cases in the upper storage floors. The basic storage structure on all floors is in this way mutually tied together and stabilized.

The total weight of each suspended unit of the revolving equipment (two double-faced revolving segments) rests on the axes of the cases and consequently on the steel girders.

The revolving segments, i.e., the movable wings of each stationary case, are fastened by a special suspension system on each side of the basic stationary unit. (In some of the structures the revolving axis is moved a few inches away from the sides of the unit.)

Access to the inner collections (two-thirds of which are, in the closed position of the compact unit, covered by the outer faces of the revolving segments) requires the opening of one of the two wings into the passages. As the revolving segments open by more than 90°, the units located at the end of the ranges extend in the full open position into the area of the side aisles, i.e., into the main communications area of the storage building.

The storage area must be equipped with a larger number of artificial lights than the non-storage area. Natural light is practically without significance because of the constant changes in the position of the revolving segments and the height of the cases.

It is evident from this description that such equipment can be used only in multi-story buildings where the main weight-bearing floor is located on the lowest level of the building. It can therefore be considered only for new buildings or for reconstructed warehouses which have been designed exclusively and permanently for specialized storage purposes.

It is, of course, theoretically possible to produce equipment of this type which could be used under less specialized circumstances.

V   The revolving compact system using the "Com-Pac-Case" equipment made by Art Metal Inc. differs from the installation described above in several respects.

Fig. 4

Examples of various double-wing compact shelving units.

[The following group of drawings is collectively referred to as Fig. 4, with the individual drawings labeled "I" through "VI". For the meaning of the letters within the drawings, see Fig. 1—Editor]

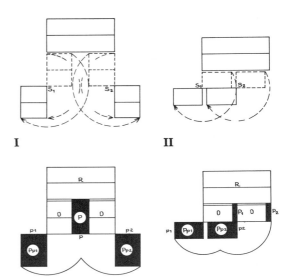

I   II

The frame structure in this system does not have to be a part of the warehouse building. The weight of the revolving segments is still supported by the stationary case, but it does not rest on only one end of the stationary case; it is divided either on both ends or at the center of the stationary case. This fact is related to another important difference—the structure of the suspended segments, which are in the form of double wings. A complete double-wing unit has at least four suspended segments. Each wing opens and closes individually, independently from the neighboring revolving segments. The suspended segments can be single-faced or double-faced. The single-faced revolving segments usually have directly accessible collections in the closed position, but upon request these cases may be supplied in a variation which places the entire collection under lock and key, in which case all collections are accessible only indirectly.

Based on the placement of the suspension, the revolving segments may open either toward the center of the stationary case (central suspension), or from the center toward the sides (side suspension). The stability of the volumes is sometimes ensured by spring braces which prevent them from spilling onto the floor when the cases are swung out.

The separation of the revolving segments into two wings makes possible a decrease in the width of the front aisles to

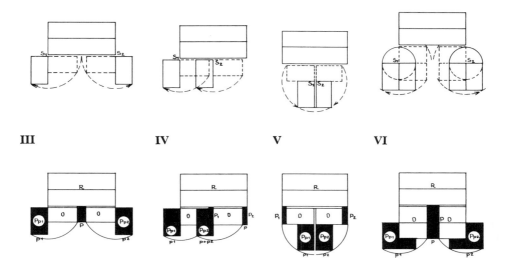

III   IV   V   VI

a standardized minimum based on safety and work regulations, i.e., a width corresponding to the passages in storage buildings using noncompact shelving.

The total obtainable capacity is, however, reduced somewhat because the combined length of the two revolving wings or segments is less than the total length of the stationary case which forms the structural frame.

VI   Let us turn our attention to the question of the actual compactness of this system of shelving equipment and to its practical application.

A Soviet specialist, the architect F. N. Pashchenko, states that a 50 to 58 percent increase in storage capacity can be achieved by the use of double-faced, and a 35 percent increase by the use of single-faced, revolving shelving, in comparison with the ordinary arrangement of double-faced stationary shelves of the standard type.[14]

The American specialist, the librarian R. H. Muller, who has made a detailed investigation of compact storage, computed that the Art Metal products make possible an increase in capacity

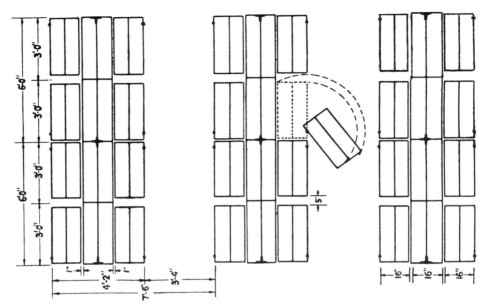

Fig. 5   *Floor plan showing an installation of single-wing,*
double-faced Snead shelving.

from 52.9 to 73.4 percent.[15] F. J. Hill, a librarian at the British Museum, states that on the basis of manufacturers' records the savings achieved with the Snead products amount to 44 to 66 percent.[16]

The West German librarian, Dr. R. Stromeyer, concludes in a special comparison of the Snead and Ingold products that the storage capacity of 1 square meter of shelving space can be increased 155 percent by a Snead installation in comparison with traditional stationary bookcases.[17]

R. T. Esterquest, the former director of the Midwest Inter-Library Center, determined that 3,150,000 volumes could be placed in the storage area of the center when specially equipped with Snead compact revolving cases, while the capacity with the use of traditional stationary cases would be only 2,090,000 volumes.[18]

The differences among the figures obtained by the individual authors are understandable since they are evaluating different products, different areas, and using different methods for computing savings or increased capacity.

As far as the various products are concerned, let us indicate some of their special differences.

According to Snead & Company data, a double-faced, six-layered single-wing unit with a 50-inch total width requires aisles 40 inches wide.

This means that instead of what is considered the minimum standard of 27 to 32 inches, it is necessary to use passages at least 40 inches wide.

The ratio of the width of area required for shelving equipment to the width required for aisles is 50:40 inches.

The minimum standard width of aisles is, however, sufficient for the double-wing cases because the length of the revolving segment is shorter than one-half of the length of the stationary case. Let us consider for example the equipment made by Art Metal. R. H. Muller states in his survey of the maximum capacity for these products that the width of a double-wing unit with four single-faced revolving segments is 36 inches, and that of a double-wing unit with four double-faced revolving segments is 48 inches. The width required for aisles with these units is 28.5 inches and 38 inches, respectively. The ratio is then 36:28.5 inches and 48:38 inches, respectively.

The necessary passage area thus differs substantially even with nearly the same area requirements for the equipment proper and the same degree of compactness. The advantage of Art Metal products over the Snead equipment, however, is decreased by the fact that the capacity of the Snead equipment is greater, although it has nearly the same dimensions as Art Metal equipment. The determination of the percentage of savings is thus influenced by the factors considered.

See the diagrams by Muller [Figs. 6 and 7] showing maximum capacity layouts using Art Metal revolving cases.

In studying these diagrams we can see that the aisles indicated are wider than that considered as the necessary minimum.

This discrepancy is caused by the fact that Muller's purpose in the preparation of the diagrams differs from the purpose of our present discussion.

Muller wants to determine the maximum use of individual types of compact shelves under the same specific storage conditions. He therefore begins with a given storage space (a unit module 23 by 23 feet) and determines the maximum attainable capacity for this space. His diagrams are of great help, but they do not provide an exact picture or exact information from the point of view of obtaining the maximum employment of individual types of equipment in various types of building construction, using different modular dimensions. This is why in the case of Art Metal products the aisle dimensions chosen are too large, because the surplus area is not sufficient for the employment of additional equipment. The same number of units of these particular products must be used in a room of smaller dimensions to achieve the maximum employment of their properties. In other words, a particular uniform modular dimension may not provide the same advantages to all types of compact shelves.

It is therefore necessary to work out for each type of equipment a separate plan for its most economical organization in all purposeful variations, and only then can we determine, on the basis of a comparison of these plans, or plans based on combinations of related equipment of various types and systems, the necessary dimensions and other properties of the space which are best in each individual case.

Even the standard comparative method is insufficient for this purpose. This method starts with the computation of the number of volumes which can be stored on shelves in a storage area of 1 square meter. It has some important disadvantages: (1) a volume as a traditional unit can be used only with the assumption that we deal with standard volumes (size, volume, weight);[19] (2) the number of volumes given for an area of 1 square meter, or even better for 1 cubic meter of space needed for the equipment, does not actually state the capacity of either the equipment itself or the total space capacity unless it is supplemented by data on the space required by those passages which are indispensable for the basic and the supplementary systems used in the organization of a particular area; (3) total capacity of a storage area cannot be established exclusively on the basis of a capacity figure based on only 1 square meter of area.

Other differences are caused by the fact that not all authors use the same basis for the computation of increased capacity or for the savings achieved.

If we wish to establish objectively the basic factors determining the degree of compactness, the most suitable method, at least for theoretical purposes, seems to be based on the computation of the ratio of area required for the equipment to the area necessary for aisles.

More exact computation would be required in evaluating individual storage constructions or renovations, which would take into consideration the exact capacity of the equipment, its cost, building construction and operating costs, and other library, technical, and economic factors which would influence

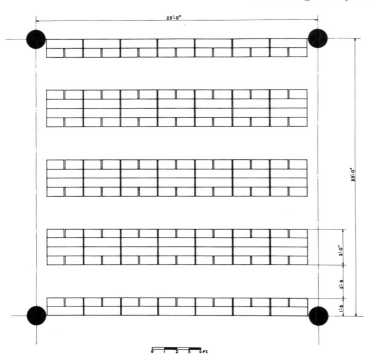

Fig. 6

*Plan by Muller I
(using Art Metal cases).*

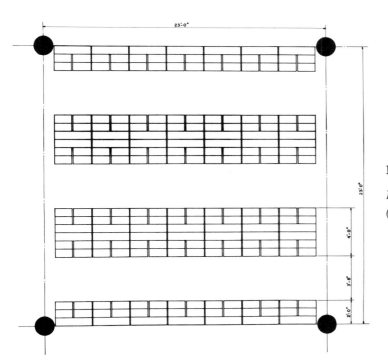

Fig. 7

*Plan by Muller II
(using Art Metal cases).*

27

the final choice in actual practice. In Czechoslovakia's planned economy, the decisions necessary to initiate the actual production of individual types of compact shelving would also have to be taken into account.

More detailed discussion will be given elsewhere.[20]

VII In order to unify the theoretical computations of the ratio of equipment area to passage area which follow, we have selected the following dimensions: single-faced shelf width for all types of revolving shelves, 25 cm.; passage width for single-wing case, 125 cm.; passage width for double-wing case, 75 cm. Case will be abbreviated as "C" and passage as "P".

An analysis of various methods of storage space organization establishes the combination of double-faced cases with supplementary single-faced cases arranged along the walls as the most efficient arrangement for revolving compact shelving. [21] The following charts and drawings illustrate this type of arrangement:

Single-faced revolving case (against wall)	Passage	Double-faced revolving case	Passage	Additional double-faced cases and passages	Single-faced revolving case (against other wall)
C	P	C	P	CP	C

←——————— Total length of storage space ———————→

Single-wing revolving segments

The following results are obtained with the employment of single-wing, single-faced compact cases (two- and four-layer units):

Example	Width of storage area	Arrangement (figures in cm.)	Ratio achieved, C to P	
			(in cm.)	(in units)
1	450 cm.	C 50 + P 125 + C 100 + P 125 + C 50	200:250	1:1.25
2	675 cm.	C 50 + P 125 + C 100 + P 125 + C 100 + P 125 + C 50	300:375	1:1.25
3	900 cm.	C 50 + P 125 + C 100 + P 125 + C 100 + P 125 + C 100 + P 125 + C 50	400:500	1:1.25

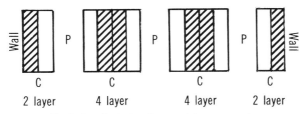

Single-faced, single-wing revolving segments

The ratio of equipment area to passage area is a constant 1:1.25.

This is a favorable ratio in comparison with stationary cases of the traditional type, where the ratio is generally 1:2, but not notably good in comparison with other systems of compact shelves.

The following results are obtained with the employment of single-wing, double-faced compact shelves (three- and six-layer units):

Example	Width of storage area	Arrangement (figures in cm.)	Ratio achieved, C to P	
			(in cm.)	(in units)
1	350 cm.	C 50 + P 75 + C 100 + P 75 + C 50	200:150	2:1.5
2	525 cm.	C 50 + P 75 + C 100 + P 75 + C 100 + P 75 + C 50	300:225	2:1.5
3	700 cm.	C 50 + P 75 + C 100 + P 75 + C 100 + P 75 + C 100 + P 75 + C 50	400:300	2:1.5
4	875 cm.	C 50 + P 75 + C 100 + P 75 + C 100 + P 75 + C 100 + P 75 + C 100 + P 75 + C 50	500:375	2:1.5

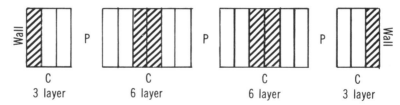

Single-wing, double-faced revolving segments

The ratio 2:1.5 is better than those obtained previously but even this ratio is not the best possible.

The following results are obtained with the employment of double-wing, double-faced (three- and six-layer units) shelves:

Example	Width of storage area	Arrangement (figures in cm.)	Ratio achieved, C to P	
			(in cm.)	(in units)
1	450 cm.	C 75 + P 75 + C 150 + P 75 + C 75	300:150	2:1
2	675 cm.	C 75 + P 75 + C 150 + P 75 + C 150 + P 75	450:225	2:1
3	900 cm.	C 75 + P 75 + C 150 + P 75 + C 150 + P 75 + C 150 + P 75 + C 75	600:300	2:1

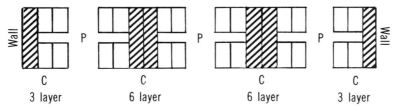

Double-wing, double-faced revolving segments

This 2:1 ratio is the maximum obtainable ratio of equipment area to passage area using the most effective type of revolving compact shelving and is the same as that obtained in computing the maximum obtainable effectiveness of drawer-type compact shelves.[22] It does not tell the whole story, however, because the total capacity of revolving equipment contained in a given area is always lower than the total capacity of drawer-type or sliding shelving covering the same area.

VIII   The computation of maximum capacity is naturally only theoretical, just as are the numerical values used in computing the ratios of the area width required for equipment to that required for aisles. Additional space is often necessary in practice for operational purposes, and the requirement for this space varies with individual libraries. The revolving compact shelves have one additional disadvantage, which has already been mentioned in general terms: the necessary shortening of the length of the revolving segments, which reduces their capacity [see Fig. 1].

According to the data of Snead & Company, this shortening of the revolving segments in two shelving units with a 6 foot total length amounts to 5 inches, or 2½ inches per segment.[23] R. Stromeyer's figures show for the same type of unit that in a unit with a stationary case 1 meter in length, the loading area of the stationary case's shelf is 9.65 cm. and that of its revolving segments, 7.95 cm. Accordingly there is a loss of 1.7 cm.

In the light of these figures, which may of course vary according to the type of the suspension device, the method of placement, and the type of movement, the value previously mentioned as the maximum obtainable effectiveness of revolving compact shelves must be reduced.

In other words, it is not possible simply to multiply the capacity of the basic stationary case by the number of supplementary revolving segments in order to determine the actual usable capacity of the total revolving equipment.

IX   We shall find in further investigation of maximum capacity in other systems of compact shelving that the degree of effectiveness can be substantially increased in some instances by the combination of several types of equipment in a single storage area. It is precisely this ability of some systems of compact shelving to be used in combination with other systems that increases their usefulness and enables a more economical organization of storage space than has been achieved up to now even in the best organized libraries.

With this thought in mind, we should avoid attempting to evaluate any type of shelving in isolation.

How does this statement affect revolving compact shelving?

A definitive answer cannot be given until we become familiar with other types and systems of compact shelving. At this time we should just mention that the ability of the present revolving compact shelving to be used in combination with other types is limited.

A combined arrangement with drawer-type shelving causes difficulties due to the fact that the revolving movement and the position of opened revolving segments make access to drawer shelves difficult. A combination with sliding shelves is possible, but the result is not any more effective than that obtained by other combinations of units.

Therefore, revolving shelving is not yet as adaptable as some other types. The successful solution of this problem would doubtless bring about increased application of this equipment, but this may require some improvement in its basic design.

In summary, let us make some basic points relating to the future production and application of revolving compact shelving in Czechoslovakia, with the reservation that the majority of these technical and operational notes have validity only under current conditions:

(a) Large-scale installations of revolving compact shelving should not be considered until after production of demonstrably more effective systems of compact shelving has begun and more detailed data and experience from the use of existing equipment abroad has been collected.

(b) Revolving compact shelving should be considered only in special conditions. At the present time, these conditions would be found only in libraries and archives in which the necessary structural features are present and would therefore not require considerable additional expense to adapt them for the new installations.

(c) The actual effectiveness of revolving compact shelving cannot be reliably tested on the basis of mere single units or small combinations. The saving of storage space cannot be fully determined on this basis, and important factors affecting operations may not be revealed. Tests of this type may at most be useful for making small structural improvements (for example in the suspension and stability of collections), or for testing loading surface capacity, weight capacity, stability, etc.

(d) Only double-wing units (either of present day or improved design) should be considered. (It will be necessary to select the dimensions for the cases and the suspension systems for both side and central suspension units which will result in the smallest loss of loading surface area.) The use of single-wing units will be practical only if we can achieve new solutions in the design which would make possible installations not requiring an increase in the standard passage width.

(e) The designing effort should concentrate on the elimination of shelving structures which are at the same time part of the building structure.

(f) Librarians should devote their attention to the investigation of actual capacity of the equipment, and, together with designers, should try to find methods that will eliminate the reduction in capacity which is one of the basic disadvantages specifically connected with this type of compact equipment.

1. Literature abroad does not contain the terms "complementary" and "independent" compact shelving. I have chosen this distinction as expressing more exactly their characteristics and as being necessary for my discussion.

2. As far as I know, the Czech terms for the individual types of compact shelving which I have decided to use are being employed in Czech professional literature for the first time. I have chosen them after careful consideration of their suitability and as a selection among several possibilities. The terms differ considerably in different languages. They range from names associated with a trademark or the name of a designer or manufacturer, to terms connected with various characteristics of the individual systems. There is no unified and definitely established terminology, even in Russian.

I am aware that I have not used a consistently applied principle: for example, the drawer-like shelving is named for the type of shelves while revolving and sliding cases are named for their type of movement. By analogy, revolving shelves should be termed "winged" or some similar term. On the other hand, drawer-type and revolving shelving is characterized as being openable, as are sliding shelves. Even the term "revolving" does not describe the nature of the units accurately because a portion of the units is stationary (non-revolving), and the movable segments "revolve" only 90°, or at most 180°. Their movement can in some measure be compared with a pendulum, and the shelving could be termed "swinging." The type of equipment described as "single-wing" and "double-wing" is also described by varying terms in foreign literature. The sliding cases, which I classify further into perpendicular and parallel sliding according to the direction of their movement, could very well be named differently. As I started to use these terms without consultation with language experts, I assume that when knowledge of this equipment becomes public, the terms will be reviewed and standardized in cooperation with specialists in professional Czech and Slovak terminology. For that reason I am planning to include in my basic work in this field, "Economical Organization of the Storage, Protection, and Use of Collections in Libraries" [not yet published], the terms used in Russian, English, French, German, Swedish, Polish, Italian, and possibly in other languages in which they are used.

3. A product of Remington Rand, described in Robert H. Muller, "Evaluation of Compact Book Storage Systems," *ACRL Monograph No. 11*, Spring, 1954, and in F. J. Hill, "The Compact Storage of Books," *Journal of Documentation*, XI (December, 1955). [Both of these articles are reprinted in this volume. See Table of Contents.]

4. Fremont Rider mentions in his book *Compact Book Storage* (New York: Hadham Press, 1949), pp. 18-28, a certain type of revolving wheel (a "Ferris wheel"), with chain-stored collections, an "elevator belt storage," and a movable "traveling crane book storage," which at first sight appear to be rather fantastic ideas as far as practical use is concerned, though they may very well be technically feasible.

5. H. Aumund, a professor at Berlin University, proposes in the book *Hebe-und Förderanlagen* (2d ed.; Berlin: Springer, 1926), Band II, 423 ff., a technically very interesting solution of movable storage space. [The storage of books on a conveyor belt system—Editor]. The proposal, however, lacks the collaboration of a professional librarian, and is perhaps a typical example of a one-sided approach as well as a proof that even what seems to be an excellent technical solution of a problem is sometimes incapable of practical application.

6. F. J. Hill, *op. cit.*, p. 202. [See page 150 of this volume.]

7. F. N. Pashchenko (Ф. Н. Пащенко), "О новых путях организации и оборудования книгохранилищ," Библиотеки ·СССР Сборник, Вып. 12 (1959), 211. [See page 125 of the Pashchenko article printed in this volume.]

8. An analysis of the advantages and the drawbacks, with practical conclusions, will be described in detail in my publication "Economical Organization of the Storage, Protection, and Use of Collections in Libraries" [not yet published].

In order to have at least an approximate idea of work time requirements in storage equipped with revolving shelves, let us mention that according to R. T. Esterquest, it takes 8½ seconds of additional work time to remove a volume from a shelf inaccessible in the basic (closed) position and about 10½ extra seconds to replace it. For removing a batch of 25 volumes, the time differential amounts to 2 minutes, 24 seconds, and for the replacement of 25 volumes, 2 minutes, 58 seconds, when compared with work in a place equipped with noncompact cases.

9. These cases had been installed in 1957 in the National Archives of the German Federal Republic, in the Roussel Laboratories in Paris, and in the city archives of La Rochelle in western France, according to data given by R. Stromeyer in *Moderne Probleme des Magazinbaues in Deutschland und seinen Nachbarländern* (Cologne: Greven Verlag, 1958), p. 70.

10. See, for example, the works by R. T. Esterquest and R. Stromeyer listed in the Bibliography.

11. R. Stromeyer, *op. cit.*, pp. 72-76.

12. See, however, the data given in R. H. Muller, *op. cit.*

13. In this connection it is instructive to note that the specialists at MILC, who had the opportunity to select from several types of compact shelving, selected the revolving cases, that the important Soviet specialist F. N. Pashchenko evidently considers revolving cases better than drawer-like shelving, and that the German specialist, librarian R. Stromeyer, apparently did not consider drawer-like shelving practical, judging from the fact that only sliding shelves (Compactus-Ingold type) and revolving shelves have been included in the analyses on which his practical conclusions have been based. I share the favorable opinions which have been expressed by Pashchenko, Stromeyer and also G. V. Meyendorf concerning sliding shelves, but on the basis of my own analysis I consider the drawer-like shelves more useful and effective than the revolving compact shelves. In order of importance for Czechoslovak products I would therefore quite definitely place perpendicular sliding shelves and drawer-like shelves before the revolving compact shelves.

14. Pashchenko, *op. cit.*, p. 211. [See page 125 of this volume.]

15. R. H. Muller, "Compact Storage Equipment," *College and Research Libraries*, XV (July, 1954), 301–302.

16. Hill, *op. cit.*, p. 210. [See page 159 of this volume.]

17. Stromeyer, *op. cit.*, p. 72.

18. Ralph T. Esterquest, "New Directions in Condensed Book Storage," *Review of Documentation*, XVIII (FID Conference, 1951), 30.

19. This was pointed out by the architect F. N. Pashchenko in his discussions with me. We share the view that the nonprofessional practice of indicating the storage capacity by the number of volumes [per cubic meter], though widely applied and still used, is indefensible.

20. See Part Three: "Sliding Drawer Compact Shelves."

21. Compare details given in Part Three.

22. Compare the data given in Part Three.

23. See Fig. 5.

Sliding Drawer Compact Shelves

I   Sliding drawer compact shelves are an entirely new type of storage equipment. The frame of sliding drawer shelving is stationary. It can, however, be either transportable or fixed, depending on the type of construction. In this sense it has some of the same properties as noncompact bookcases of the standard type. The loading surface itself—the drawer-like shelf—is movable. The combination of a stationary frame and a movable shelf makes possible the creation of a completely new type of compact shelving installation.

In its structure the shelving of this compact system differs more than any other shelving from the traditional stationary storage cases because its basic element, the loading surface, is designed on principles different from those employed in other shelving, whether of compact or noncompact design.

As a matter of fact, its only similarity to conventional shelving, whether of the cabinet type, or the open-frame type which is so widely used in libraries and archives, is the stationary frame. But even the frame of at least the cabinet type of sliding drawer shelving has an outward appearance which resembles more the frame of a vertical file drawer than it does the traditional cabinet type of shelving. The open-frame structure of traditional bookcases can, however, be applied successfully in some cases to this type of compact shelving.

The most radical change from the other systems of storage equipment is in the structural design of the shelves. Regular plain shelves are replaced by sliding drawer shelves which are similar to the drawers in vertical file cabinets. These shelves have all the advantages of well-constructed drawers. They are equipped with ball-bearings to make opening and closing them easy. They can be removed and transferred from one frame to another, but are secured against falling out when fully extended. In use, whether they are fully or only partially loaded with books, the shelves remain in a perfectly horizontal position; they can be locked; and their height can be adjusted to correspond to various book sizes. Various forms of shelves are available. There is the so-called double-head variety, in which each drawer slides open in both directions, and also the single-head variety, with one-directional sliding drawers. The loading surfaces can be designed for a two-way placement in which the books are all arranged in two rows parallel to the sides of the drawer shelves, or in a three-way placement. In the latter, the drawer has a partition about one-third or one-fourth of the distance from its front. In the front part, the books are placed across the width of the drawer; in the back part, they are placed in two rows parallel to the sides in a double-faced arrangement. The three-way drawers are open in front so that the volumes placed in the front row are accessible even in the drawer's closed position, and are therefore as directly accessible as those in noncompact systems. The drawers have very low side walls, or sometimes no side walls, in which case the side walls are not part of the movable drawer, but are formed by the solid frame structure or the bracing between drawers. The shelves come in several widths, roughly corresponding to the widths of ordinary shelves. In length, the shelves are usually shorter than regular bookcase shelves, but there is a drawer shelf in existence, the length of which exceeds the usual center-to-center distance of double-faced units (125 cm.). Of course, this is a double-head drawer shelf designed to slide in both directions so as not to require the aisle width that would otherwise be necessary.

Sliding drawer shelves offer the same possibilities for various systems of placement and storage of the collections as do stationary cases of the standard type. The volumes can be stored by the method which is commonly used in libraries and archives, i.e., with their spines in vertical or horizontal position facing the user, or the method suggested by Rider with their spines in horizontal position facing upward, or by V. A. Marin's method with spines in vertical position across the shelf width on stationary shelves, and along the length in drawer-like shelves.

According to manufacturers, the collections in sliding-drawer compact shelves can be stored with complete safety, and their stability is nearly as secure as in traditional cases when the correct operating procedures are followed. They emphasize that installations are successful even in those libraries where the readers have free access to the collections.

The degree of compactness which can be attained with this type of shelving is increased by the possibility of the complete removal of the unproductive transverse or cross passages which are a substantial source of decreased capacity in storage systems with stationary shelving and by a more efficient organization of the total storage area with passages only along the front side of the drawers. The width of frontal passages can be of minimum standard dimensions, the same as those used in storage spaces equipped with the traditional stationary shelving. The space considered necessary for operational purposes and safety standards in traditional types of storage areas is usually sufficient for the drawers in their open position. This is not true, however, in certain cases, such as in the storage area of libraries with a substantial amount of traffic, where the width of the aisles must be increased for reasons of communication and efficient operation, or, of course, in installations in which the length of one-directional drawers exceeds the standard passage width.

Sliding drawer compact shelves are used most widely in the United States. Hamilton Compo Stacks and the Ames Stor-Mor Book Drawers are the best known types.

II   V. A. Marin has successfully applied the principle of sliding drawers in the Soviet Union. The most significant feature of the Soviet design is the adaptability of the drawers and frames to a very wide range of book sizes. The width and height dimensions of drawers are adjustable to the needs resulting from the standardization of sizes found in Soviet publications.[1]

The Soviet specialist F. N. Pashchenko does not, however, consider this type of compact shelving as suitable for general application in the operations of Soviet libraries.[2] He objects to its relatively complex structure and its bulkiness, and states that its effectiveness does not equal that of simpler and less expensive compact shelving installations.[3] He admits, however, that this type could be utilized successfully in the remodeling of older storage areas. This has already been verified by research and by experimental tests undertaken by V. A. Marin. Marin's experiment was made in connection with the proposed reconstruction of the storage area of the "Russian Collection" in the Saltykov-Shchedrin Library in Leningrad. There, the compact storage of the collection with book sizes up to 20 cm. (7.874 inches) in sliding drawer shelves would more than double the capacity obtained by traditional storage methods.[4]

III   The sliding drawer compact shelving known as "Hamilton Compo Stack" consists of a special solid frame structure and movable drawer shelves equipped with ball-bearings. The frame (in its present production model) apparently cannot be replaced by any current frame used in standard stationary shelving. The sliding drawers of this model possess special characteristics. The drawers are produced in several sizes. They vary in length from 36 to 48 inches, and come in widths of 18, 22, or 26 inches. The drawer height is adjustable and can be changed to fit the size of the collections because the carriage frames are grooved horizontally. The drawers are single-headed and slide out into the aisles in one direction only. The front part of the drawer is open, without a front panel, and books in this section are placed with their spines facing outward along the width of the drawer. Part of the collection is therefore directly accessible in a way similar to collections placed on

Fig. 8

Structure of Hamilton Compo Stacks.

Fig. 9

Sliding drawer shelf.
Hamilton Compo Stack.

Fig. 10   *Storage area with Hamilton Compo Stack shelving.*

the shelves of traditional stationary cases. Nearly one-third of the collections can be arranged in this position, depending on the proportional width of the drawers. The remaining books are placed on both sides along the length of the drawer from the partition separating the front section to the rear of the drawer. These books are accessible only when the drawer is pulled open. The advantage of this arrangement is that at least a portion of the collections can be used under conditions equal to normal conditions in other types of installations. However, since the total content of the drawer is not ranged along a single edge, as it would be on a standard bookcase shelf, but must be approached from one of three sides, the withdrawal or replacement of a book may require up to three operational steps. Considering that in a standard stationary 1 meter case, 6 or 7 shelves are accessible from one direction (i.e., 18 to 21 times the number of books accessible from one direction in a three-way drawer), it is clear that the work in a storage place equipped with sliding drawer shelves of this type is more demanding. It is more demanding even when the two-way, double-faced sliding drawer shelves are used. This disadvantage of drawer-type compact shelving can be at least partially offset by proper markings on tags or labels fastened to the drawer fronts and by orientational diagrams showing the location of collections in the storage area; both of these procedures are therefore used more systematically by workers in compact storage areas than by those in conventional storage areas.

IV   The compact sliding drawer shelves made by the W. R. Ames Company have a somewhat simpler frame construction. Also, according to the information supplied by the manufacturer, and verified in practice, frames of existing standard cases can be used with this equipment. It is possible to remove the shelves currently used in old storage areas and replace them in the same frames with the sliding drawer shelves of the "Stor-Mor" make. The standard frame structure must, however, be strong enough (or must be susceptible enough to structural strengthening) to support the increased load.[5] This interchangeability of frames is no doubt the reason for F. N. Pashchenko's recommendation to Soviet libraries to take advantage of sliding drawer shelving in the reconstruction of old storage areas.

42

The W. R. Ames Company employs a common frame structure for its "Stor-Mor" equipment and for its "Multi-tier" equipment. The latter is designed to be used in a system with combined stationary and compact shelving.

The Ames "Stor-Mor" sliding drawer shelves differ sustantially from the "Hamilton Compo Stack" shelves. The former approximate the shape of ordinary shelves, but are "double-headed" and slide out into the aisle on either side of the frame. Drawers of this type are approximately double the standard length and come in two sizes, 68⅝ inches and 76⅝ inches. The drawer fronts are 7⅝ inches high. The drawer width, which is approximately 18 inches (or one-half the length of a stationary double-faced bookcase) makes possible an arrangement in which two adjacent drawers take up a space of approximately 3 feet (i.e., the total length of a standard stationary bookcase), thus making it possible

Fig. 11   *Ames Stor-Mor Book Drawers.*

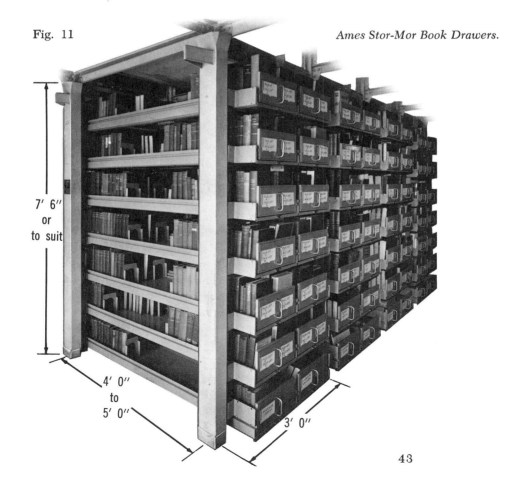

7' 6"
or
to suit

4' 0"
to
5' 0"

3' 0"

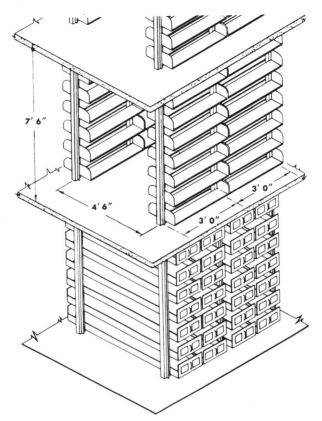

Fig. 12

*Multi-tier storage structure
with both compact shelving
and stationary shelving
of the traditional type.*

to utilize existing stationary shelving frames for the installation
of these drawers.

Another difference is in the complete double-faced arrangement of books, which are all placed on the two sides along the
length of the drawers. The drawer slides keep the loading surface
permanently in horizontal position, and this is considerably
easier than in the case of the "Hamilton Compo Stack" drawers,
because when an Ames drawer is pulled out in one direction,
the complete second half of the drawer still remains in the supporting grooves and acts as a counterbalance. The shelves slide
on ball-bearings. Each drawer of the "Stor-Mor" shelves when
closed is secured by a positive-locking catch.

As the collections are arranged in the drawers to face in only
two directions, the "Stor-Mor" equipment lacks the advantage
of any direct access, and books are accessible only when the
drawers are pulled open.

The content of the drawers is indicated on 3- by 5-inch cards which are inserted in a frame provided on the face of all drawers.

The degree of compactness and the savings in storage area with this equipment are basically the same as in a "Hamilton Compo Stack" installation when the Hamilton equipment is used in an arrangement accessible from two aisles, i.e., the paired arrangement which will be discussed in Section VI, below.

V   Because of the "double-head" form of the drawers, the "Stor-Mor" system is suitable only for a storage area which contains at least two parallel aisles. The best utilization of the storage space, as will be demonstrated later, can be achieved only in a combined system, for example, the "Stor-Mor," together with "Hamilton Compo Stacks" or other type of shelving which can be placed in a single row along the walls and thus serve as an economically effective supplement.

The employment of "Hamilton Compo Stacks" alone, on the other hand, is effective for a very narrow storage area with a long axis (one aisle is sufficient, i.e., a minimum width of one range and one aisle), in which the sections can be placed with their closed side along one or both of the longer walls of the room. It is important to notice this feature which, together with the advantage of having nearly one-third of the collection directly accessible, is without doubt very important in the evaluation of suitable applications of the Hamilton type of sliding drawer compact shelves.

VI   It seems desirable now to formulate more precisely the plan proposed in general form by F. N. Pashchenko concerning the most compact arrangement of storage areas possible with sliding drawer shelving using the stationary frames of existing shelving.[6]

It is also desirable to complement this plan with further variations which may come to mind when investigating the suitability of certain methods of organization under various storage conditions.

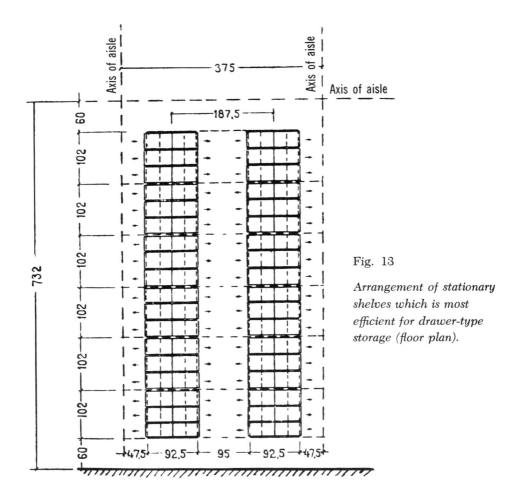

Fig. 13

Arrangement of stationary shelves which is most efficient for drawer-type storage (floor plan).

For the purpose of considering this plan (in which consideration all other factors normally considered by a librarian in making practical decisions about the choice of equipment have been eliminated) it is unnecessary to make computations based on exact dimensions and sizes of the existing foreign products. Various sizes of equipment can often be adjusted to the dimensions of the stationary bookcases found in old libraries or to the designs of individual manufacturers. The exact numerical dimensions are not necessary to conduct a valid investigation of the suitability of various systems (though they are of course very important for the architect, project manager, builder, and librarian in making their decisions on a particular project since these decisions must take into account technical questions of construction, as well as the exact organization of a given storage

46

area). However, the ratio between the area required for the equipment and that required for aisles is vitally important. Thus it is quite sufficient for our purposes that we express at least this ratio correctly in exact figures as long as we are trying to solve only the question of maximum capacity for typical installations.[7] In fact, detailed computations using exact data for various shelving sizes would serve no practical purpose in Czechoslovakia, where there is no current production of sliding drawer compact shelving, and where no decisions have been made about sizes in any possible future manufacture.

For these reasons we shall arbitrarily use the following unit dimensions in our diagrams and computations: aisle width, 75 cm.; sliding drawer cases accessible from one aisle [single-head], 75 cm.; sliding drawer cases accessible from two aisles [double-head], 150 cm.[8]

The installations marked Variations A and B [Figs. 14 and 15] represent an arrangement of [single-head] sliding drawer cases accessible from one aisle, placed in a storage area of a minimum width, with a single aisle.

The arrangement shown in Variation A requires an equipment area 75 cm. wide and an aisle 75 cm. wide. The ratio of equipment area to aisle area is therefore 1:1.

This arrangement can be used in a storage room 150 cm. wide.

The arrangement shown in Variation B requires an equipment area 75 cm. + 75 cm. wide and a passage 75 cm. wide. The ratio is twice as good (2:1).

This arrangement can be used in a storage room 225 cm. wide.

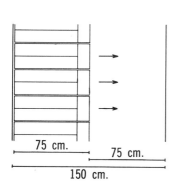

Fig. 14   *Variation A.*

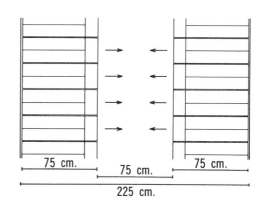

Fig. 15   *Variation B.*

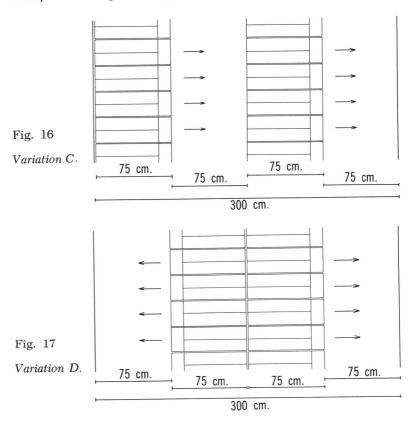

Fig. 16

Variation C.

Fig. 17

Variation D.

The installations shown as Variations C and D [Figs. 16 and 17] contain an arrangement of [single-head] sliding drawer shelves accessible from two aisles, placed in a storage area of minimum width, and with two parallel aisles.

The width of the area is the same in both of these variations— 300 cm.

Variation C shows a nonpaired system of shelving sections. Paired shelving sections with one-directional [single-head] drawers are shown in Variation D. Of course in Variation D the same results would be obtained from systems equipped with [double-head] drawers that slide in opposite directions as for systems with one-directional drawers.

In both Variations C and D the width of the area required for equipment comes to 150 cm. ($C = 75 + 75$; $D = 150$), and the total passage width is also 150 cm. ($75 + 75$) in both examples.

The ratio is therefore the same as in Variation A (1:1).

It is evident, then, that *there is no advantage in a paired [two ranges, back-to-back] arrangement used in a storage area which has a capacity for only two shelf ranges and two passages.*

Such an advantage is available only in storage areas which are wider. This fact is evident from the following table:

Total width of area (in cm.)	Number of shelf ranges	Number of aisles	Total equipment area (in cm.)	Total aisle area (in cm.)	Ratio of equipment to aisle	Equip- ment	Aisle
						percentage	
300	2	2	150	150	1:1	50	50
525	4	3	300	225	2:1.5	57	43
750	6	4	450	300	2:1.33	60	40
975	8	5	600	375	2:1.25	61.6	38.4
1,200	10	6	750	450	2:1.20	62.5	37.5
1,425	12	7	900	525	2:1.17	63.2	36.8
1,650	14	8	1,050	600	2:1.14	63.6	36.4

The ratio remains constant at 1:1 in further variations of a nonpaired arrangement; it becomes progressively more advantageous in a paired arrangement as the width of the area increases (but in no case does it reach a 2:1 ratio).

Other conclusions may be drawn. Storage areas sufficiently wide for only two ranges of sliding drawer shelving are not advantageous as far as maximum use of space is concerned unless they have only one central passage, as in Variation B, because otherwise, no ratio better than 1:1 can be obtained, whether a paired arrangement is used or not.

Therefore, for a storage area just wide enough to contain two ranges of sliding drawer shelving, the nonpaired arrangement with a common central passage is best, and results in a 2:1 ratio, which is the maximum ratio obtainable with this type of compact shelving.

This ratio can also be achieved in storage areas which have a capacity of 4 or more ranges of shelving by a combined arrangement of paired and nonpaired ranges. An example is shown in Variation E [Fig. 18].

By this method of combining paired and nonpaired ranges it is possible to place in an area 450 cm. wide the same number of ranges which in an uncombined, nonpaired arrangement would require a width of 525 cm. (with 3 passages) or 600 cm. (with 4 passages), and in an uncombined, paired arrangement (with 4 passages), a width of 525 cm.

A plan for maximum capacity of a storage area equipped with sliding drawer compact shelving must be based on the principle of a combined arrangement. R. H. Muller's plan for the organization of a storage area equipped with "Hamilton Compo Stack" shelving serves as an example [Fig. 19]. This plan is, of course, not valid for all the different types of sliding drawer shelving manufactured today, but it can be used for those shelves which are suitable.

We should mention here that the maximum obtainable ratio of 2:1, with a nonpaired arrangement as shown in Variation B, is an exception which applies exclusively to a storage area of minimum width (225 cm.) Any further enlargement of the storage area width must result in changing the organization of the area into the combined arrangement described above.

Fig. 18   *Variation E.*

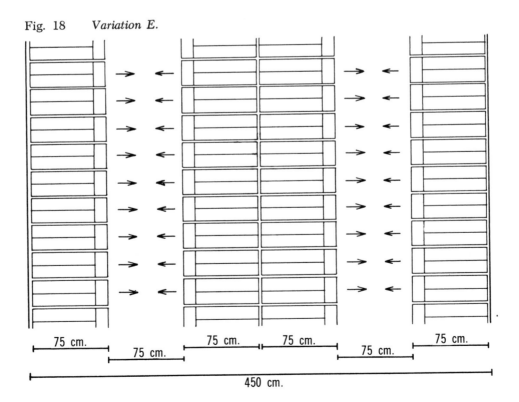

75 cm.   75 cm.   75 cm.   75 cm.   75 cm.   75 cm.   75 cm.

450 cm.

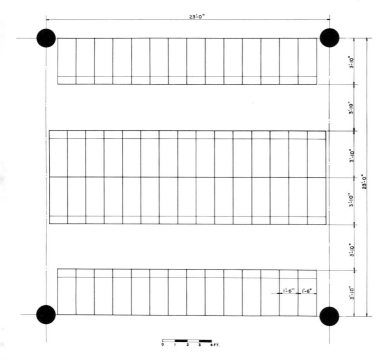

Fig. 19

Diagram of maximum capacity of a storage area equipped with Hamilton Compo Stack shelving.

This arrangement is the result of a combination of Variations B and D where the type B arrangement is used as a supplement to the main installation.

VII   These computations and diagrams of maximum capacity, as well as the numerical ratios of equipment width to passage width, are understandably only theoretical. In practice, each storage area with more than one aisle running parallel to the ranges may need to contain at least one connecting cross passage running perpendicular to the ranges, or possibly two cross passages, one at each end of the system.

An advantage of a storage arrangement with a cross passage at the far end of the range system is that a librarian can withdraw and replace volumes located in that portion of the storage room more than half the length of the room away from the service counter without the necessity of returning all the way in order to enter another aisle. In this way, communication is substantially shortened. Two cross passages are indispensable in those libraries which do not have individual openings or doors leading into each storage room aisle.

It is to be understood that computations (including many different factors) are necessary in each individual case when trying to determine the best practical use of a particular storage area.

It should be added that the best possible ratio, 2:1, which is certainly good in comparison with the usual 1:2 ratio for stationary storage equipment, is still not the best possible when compared with other compact storage systems—in some of which substantially better ratios are obtainable.

VIII   The achievement of this maximum 2:1 ratio, which, as previously pointed out, is a constant if we choose the combined arrangement, also depends on a correct ratio of the length of the shelving equipment to the width of the aisles. This ratio should be 1:1. The ratio cannot be improved as far as the equipment is concerned because drawers longer than the width of the passage could not be opened completely. On the other hand, if the aisles are wider than necessary to open the drawers full length, the storage effectiveness is reduced because there is proportionately less area available for the storage of collections. Therefore we can see that the best choice for the length of the shelves should be that which coincides with the width of the passages. However, a decision as to the maximum size of the complete installation (taking into consideration, for example, the widened main communication aisles which are required by operational necessities in some libraries) is not to be made from a purely theoretical point of view, but must also take into consideration the questions of storage capacity, the particular kind of equipment, production problems, the use of the collection, and operational procedures.

When the maximum capacity and the conditions for its achievement are determined, we should still pose the question as to whether the results obtained are the best possible.

Could not the sliding drawer compact shelving be used still more effectively?

We have not found answers to this question in the data supplied by the manufacturers, who naturally do not omit any of the advantages of the equipment in their descriptions, whether these advantages are real or are only ascribed to the products for advertising purposes. The same dearth of this kind of information unfortunately exists in discussions among professional people and in the professional literature.

In our opinion, however, there is a way in which the shelving can be used more effectively.

The improvement in effectiveness is based on an arrangement of the storage area using sliding drawer shelves in combination with compact shelving of other types.

(1) If we use a system composed of drawer-type shelving and of sliding bookcases with a lateral [parallel sliding] movement, the improvement will amount to roughly 33⅓ percent because the original 75 cm. drawers can, in effect, be lengthened by approximately 25 cm. [see Fig. 20].

(2) If we use a system composed of drawer-type shelving and sliding bookcases 1 meter long with a frontal [perpendicular] movement, the drawers can, in effect, be lengthened a total of 100 cm. This amounts to an improvement of 133 percent [see Fig. 21]. If we use our previously accepted dimensions

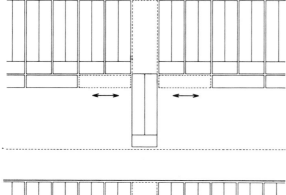

Fig. 20

Combination of drawer-type and parallel sliding bookcases.

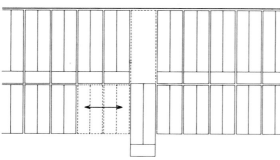

Fig. 21

Combination of drawer-type and perpendicular sliding bookcases.

for equipment and passages, we can now obtain a ratio of 175:75. This ratio is very favorable even in comparison with other compact shelving systems which, when used by themselves, would ordinarily be more effective than sliding drawer compact shelving used by itself.

Theoretically, there are other advantageous possibilities, some of which, however, would probably require some structural improvements in either the drawer-type shelving or the sliding bookcases, or both.

IX   In conclusion we would like to list the requirements that should be applied to any future Czechoslovak production of drawer-type shelving. We shall list only those special requirements which differ from the general requirements placed on compact shelving of all types.

(a) The frame structure should be as simple as possible. The adaptability of the equipment to fit the frames of common stationary cases, however, is not an indispensable condition because the number of libraries which would be considered for such a remodeling in Czechoslovakia is small.

(b) The span of load-bearing frame standards and supports between drawers should be adjustable to shelves of various widths. A universal frame construction, adaptable to use with sections of different sizes, would be advantageous.

(c) Drawer slides equipped with ball-bearings should be adjustable.

This would make possible an adjustment in the height of the drawer space according to book sizes. Such an arrangement can be easily designed with the help of horizontal grooving of the load-bearing and bracing partitions between drawers.

(d) There is an advantage in producing both the single-head and the double-head drawer shelves in that this would ensure the possibility of using combined arrangements of shelving systems.

(e) The size of shelves should be standardized. The width dimensions must be adjusted to fit standard book sizes. The length of shelves should be standardized, preferably 75 cm. for drawers [single-head] sliding in one direction and 150 cm. for drawers [double-head] sliding in two directions.

(f) The front portion, the "head" of the sliding drawer, in both the single- and double-headed version should be open for the placement of directly accessible collections. The stability of the books should be ensured by mechanical means.

(g) Synthetic materials can be substituted for metal in the loading surface.

(h) The majority of our storage areas can use an open frame construction without a locking arrangement. A solid cabinet-type lockable construction will be necessary for some types of rooms and for certain types of collections (valuable archives, manuscripts, first editions, rare books, and other special collections). Proper atmospheric conditions for collections placed in such bookcases can be ensured by the use of perforated cases and suitable controls over temperature, humidity, and the circulation of air.

X   This relatively detailed description of drawer-type shelving and of its properties does not mean that we advocate its massive use in all our libraries and archives. It is presented in order to offer complete basic information on new types of shelving used abroad. Its properties are described so that we can form a clear idea of its suitability for use here in Czechoslovakia. In practice, we shall doubtless weigh carefully all the advantages and disadvantages of drawer-type shelving, both by itself and in comparison with other compact systems.

As far as the ability to mass produce such equipment is concerned, we believe that in Czechoslovakia, with its highly developed industry and its well-known technical skills, the question need not even arise.

However, the manufacture of prototypes and the testing of products is quite indispensable and should be started without delay.

The question of patent licensing to begin mass production may be a problem for a short period of time. It should not be difficult to verify our actual need for such equipment, and it would be incorrect to assume that this need will be limited to Czechoslovak libraries, archives, and similar installations.

The prime requirements are the speeding up of the production of the necessary prototypes, the testing of their properties, and the gaining of reliable experience from practical applications.

1. V. A. Marin and A. A. Songina(В. А. Марин, и А. А. Сонгина), Определение габаритов стеллажей компактного хранения, Ленинград: 1958.

2. F. N. Pashchenko (Ф. Н. Пащенко), "О новых путях организации и оборудования книгохранилиш," Библиотеки СССР Сборник. Вып. 12 (1959), 209–10. [See page 124 of this volume.]

3. Detailed analyses of the effectiveness of individual types of compact shelving and of combined arrangements of stationary and movable shelving will be given in my proposed publication "Economical Organization of Storage, Protection, and Use of Collections in Libraries." Data about costs of the principal types of storage areas were published by Robert H. Muller in "Evaluation of Compact Book Storage Systems," *ACRL Monograph No. 11,* Spring, 1954. They were reprinted by F. J. Hill in "The Compact Storage of Books," *Journal of Documentation,* XI (December, 1955), which also includes costs for English libraries.

4. V. A. Marin (В. А. Марин), Компактное хранение библиотечных фондов странах Западной Европы и Америки, Ленинград: 1957. стройопис (typescript).

5. In Czechoslovakia this has been done in the State Technical Library in Brno, in the Matica Slovenská in Martin, and in the Library of the National Museum in Prague.

6. F. N. Pashchenko, *op. cit.,* p. 210. [See page 124 of this volume.]

7. Data on maximum capacities of specific makes of equipment are given by R. H. Muller, *op. cit.*
   The maximum capacity of all types of shelving will be examined in detail in my proposed publication, "Economical Organization, Storage, Protection and Use of Collections in Libraries," which will also contain analyses, tables, and all basic diagrams.

8. The dimensions were selected because they have, in our opinion, some important properties which could be successfully applied in Czechoslovak products. These dimensions represent the lower size limit of the sliding drawer-like shelving suitable for the maximum use of a storage area capacity, as is pointed out later in the text.

PART FOUR

Sliding (Rolling) Compact Shelves

I   When a person sees a compactly organized storage area equipped exclusively with sliding compact shelving for the first time, he receives the impression that he is confronted with something entirely new, an installation that has almost nothing in common with a storage area equipped with traditional stationary bookcases.

A traditional storage room area is lined along the sides by single-faced stationary bookcases and subdivided by criss-crossing communication aisles within which sections of double-faced stationary bookcases are scattered.

Although the whole area should serve a unified purpose, it is differentiated "functionally"; and although all the bookcases belong together organically, they are split up, as often as not, in a haphazard manner.

The area is frequently illuminated by artificial light in the center and natural light at the sides; the two types of lighting, combined with the network of aisles, create an atmosphere submerged half in light and half in shadow.

In contrast, the space in a well organized compact storage area equipped with sliding shelves is organized neatly into two compact blocks connected either by one T- or by one H-shaped avenue of communication, depending on the aisle arrangement.

However, if we examine the sliding compact equipment in more detail, we can see that its basic unit is nothing but the traditional solid bookcase, and its basic principles are the same as in the systems of drawer-type and revolving compact shelves.

Even the most modern and efficiently designed products which differ the most from stationary bookcases and impart to a compact storage area completely new properties, are actually neither structurally nor operationally independent from the traditional bookcases. On the contrary, in all the products we can distinctly trace the gradual development from the basic type of bookcase which has characterized libraries and archives for four centuries. The new products represent the highest development of the original equipment, but are also subject to its limitations, both now and in the future.

The first sliding shelves came into being under the same conditions as the first revolving shelves. They were at first used only as complementary adjuncts to stationary shelves, and only later were some of them transformed into separate sliding equipment usable independently from those shelves.

The direct motive for their construction was an effort to utilize the unnecessarily large aisles in the storerooms of some old libraries. This effort led to the creation of the revolving shelf protoype used in the Bradford Free Library, which was described in Part Two. It led also to the creation of movable shelves which slid out parallel to their length, a principle used even before World War I by the London firm W. Lucy and Co. for the equipment installed in the renowned Bodleian Library at Oxford, and later in the Cambridge University Library. Shelves sliding in the direction parallel to their length became the basis for the drawer-like sliding shelves and also influenced the other types of movable shelves.

The methods used to solve the problem of utilizing this unnecessary aisle space then developed in three directions. The first two methods resulted in the revolving shelves and the drawer-type sliding compact shelves which have already been partially described.[1] This section will deal with the third method and its basic variations.

The best example of the original type of sliding bookcases about which reliable information has been preserved is represented by the cases in the British Museum in London.

II   A so-called sliding cabinet type of bookcase was used in the gallery storage area of the Iron Library of the British Museum to supplement the original system of stationary shelves. These cases slid on overhead rails in a direction parallel to the ranges of stationary shelves, in front of which they were placed. The center-to-center distance of the original cases in the Iron Library was not unnecessarily large, and the movable cases were placed in the front passages along one side only of the stationary cases. They were added irregularly according to the needs of growing collections in individual sections of the library. Another characteristic was the spacing of the movable cases, which were not placed in front of the stationary ranges in a continuous row, but were placed in such a way as to leave alternate spaces between them into which a case could be moved to gain access to the stationary shelves covered by it in its original position.

Fig. 22   *Supplementary sliding cases.*
a — *original stationary case*   b — *parallel sliding case*
———→ *direction of movement*

Increase in storage capacity obtained by this method obviously was not very large, but apparently the equipment proved successful in use. The principal advantages of this kind of arrangement are its low cost and its easy installation, which can be made in stages according to actual operational needs. Practical use of the Iron Library bookcases did not present any particular difficulties. No trouble was encountered as long as the guide mechanism was kept in good condition and the books were placed in such a manner that they would not be damaged by the movement of the cases. The equipment was removed in 1920 during the reconstruction of the storage areas of the British Museum; the slotted cast iron floors from which the sliding cases were hung were removed because of their unsatisfactory load-bearing capacity.

Note: The terms "parallel sliding bookcases" and "perpendicular sliding bookcases" are used throughout the book to describe the movement of the cases in relation to the long direction of their shelves. The "parallel sliding" case slides in a direction parallel to the length of its shelves, and the "perpendicular sliding" case moves in a direction perpendicular to the length of its shelves.

Sliding shelves used as complementary equipment for stationary shelves found application later in various new constructions of parallel sliding shelves, not only in Britain and the United

States, but also in Sweden after World War II. The main interest in their improvement was for the purpose of achieving increased compactness in the new combined systems. Movable cases were placed on both sides of the original double-faced stationary case in a single or even a double row. The equipment of this type was known as the "Stormor" type. The English company J. Glover and Sons, Ltd. of London supplied the Royal Library in Stockholm after World War II with this type of equipment which provided an increase in capacity of 63 to 65 percent. The same type of equipment was installed in the University Library in Uppsala. Another London firm (Acrow Ltd.) produced a special type of shelves for the "Stormor" system, which were then used in several British libraries.

In Sweden these movable cases have been in production since 1952 by the firm E. A. Rosengren AB in Gothenburg.

III   We also want to follow a second line of development which led to the design of independent parallel sliding cases. In this connection we should remember one of the oldest designs, the one proposed by Gladstone for the British Museum [see Hill, Appendix E, page 149]. The important part of his design was the proposal for the use of all former frontal passage areas for the placement of equipment and the enlargement of the function of the cross passages which formerly served only for communications.[2]

In systems of independent parallel sliding cases the movable cases are placed in the area of former frontal passages. The stationary cases are also completely replaced by movable cabinet type cases. The movable cases, placed side by side, are provided with wheels and slide out into one common transverse passage. The collections stored on the shelves are accessible only when the bookcase slides out from the closed position into this transverse passage.

The saving in the area of the former frontal passages is partially reduced by the necessary enlargement of the transverse passage to more than the standard width; this passage must be at least as wide as the length of the movable compact case.

Double-faced cases of this type were produced around 1931 by the English firm of T. E. Foulkes for the British Museum. The cases were of steel frame construction, 7 feet high and 3 feet 7

60

inches long, and were suspended on rollers which moved on steel beams at the ceiling level. The bookcases were arranged in ranges of 14 to 16 units.

Parallel sliding bookcases of the same type, the so-called Vernier mobile bookstack, were produced by another London company (Libraco) for the Mitchell Library in Glasgow. One hundred and fifty-eight bookcase units, supplemented by stationary cases along the walls, were installed in this library in a storage area of 2,100 square feet. The original capacity of this area with traditional stationary shelving was 44,640 volumes. The installation of compact sliding equipment made possible an increase to 81,000 volumes.

Similar but structurally simpler parallel sliding cases were already being produced in 1930 by Snead & Company for the Toronto Public Library in Canada. These open-type cases move on wheels, and without rails. Special preparatory installation is unnecessary as long as the floor is hard, smooth, and level. Double-faced cases are 100 cm. (3.281 feet) long. The passage is approximately 120 cm. (3.937 feet) wide. The head librarian, H. C. Campbell, states that the installation, which has been used

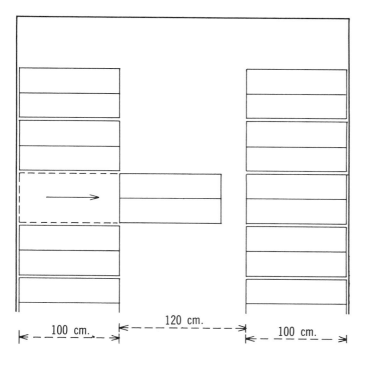

Fig. 23

Parallel sliding cases. (Toronto)

Fig. 24

*Parallel sliding
cases. (Toronto)*

for many years, is entirely successful.[3] The savings amount to
approximately 33 percent of the storage area.

The first prototypes and test series of parallel sliding bookcases for compact storage in Czechoslovakia were used in the
library of the Military Political Academy in Prague. (For details
of this installation see Part Five, pages 104-106.)

IV Parallel sliding compact bookcases are composed
structurally from a standard solid double-faced (or sometimes a
single-faced) cabinet-type or open-type bookcase, with a movable wheel-type or roller-type undercarriage, or with a suspension
system.

They can therefore be classified by their type of sliding gear as either wheel- or roller-bookcases, which slide on rails or freely on the floor, or as suspended movable bookcases.

The movement is always in the direction parallel to the length of the shelves. Movement is made manually.

If we compare parallel sliding compact cases with the shelving of other compact systems, we can see that in principle they are closest to the drawer-type compact shelves. They share the same limitations of access to the collections, and their method of placement is similar.

The main structural difference is in the frame, which is stationary in drawer-type bookcases while the individual shelves are movable; in parallel sliding cases the frame is movable and the shelves are not.

Their operational properties are nearly identical, both when they are used alone, or in combined systems.

The collections in independent systems of parallel sliding bookcases are placed in the same manner as on the shelves of the stationary cases, but they are not directly accessible until the shelves are pulled out into the aisles. In our opinion, a three-sided placement could be considered after a restyling of the loading surface. A detailed proposal will be introduced in our evaluation of perpendicular sliding bookcases.

V   The equipment which was installed in the British Museum can also be used as a model in describing another type of sliding bookcase, the perpendicular sliding bookcase. This type has developed from the original supplementary type into the most effective independent type of compact equipment.

Supplementary bookcases, which differed from the type introduced into the Iron Library, were installed in the British Museum in the 1890's. They were double-faced movable bookcases of the same size as the original stationary cases. The movable bookcases were suspended on rails in an iron carrier device with clamping screws. The books stored in the front face of the movable bookcase were directly accessible. Books placed on the inside of the movable case and the books on the shelves of the stationary cases behind it were accessible only after the sliding case was moved away. The sliding movement went in the direction perpendicular to the frontal passage.

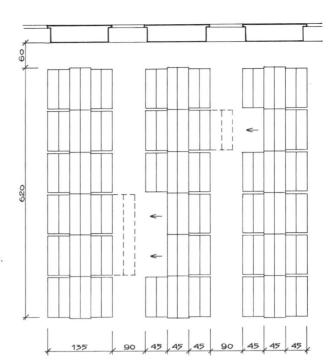

Fig. 25

*Diagram of a compact
installation with stationary
cases and supplementary
perpendicular sliding cases.*

Fig. 26   *Sliding compact bookcases of the suspension type in the storage area
of the British Museum (supplementary equipment used until 1920).*

Both the advantages and disadvantages mentioned in our description of parallel sliding cases used in the Iron Library apply in the main to this equipment as well.

This equipment was removed in 1920 in the remodeling which, it should be noted, was done to replace the unsuitable cast iron floors, and not because of any deficiencies in the equipment itself.

VI   When we consider that librarians and manufacturers have had experience with independent parallel sliding cases (in Toronto, in the British Museum, in Glasgow, etc.), and with supplementary perpendicular sliding equipment (British Museum), and have thus had the chance to evaluate their practical advantages and disadvantages, it is not surprising that the production of equipment which would combine the advantages and reduce the disadvantages of both systems was not long in coming. The parallel sliding bookcases, as we mentioned previously, pointed the way for the removal of frontal passages, and contributed to a substantial increase in compactness of storage areas when the equipment is in its basic (closed) position. The

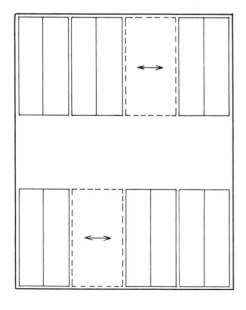

Fig. 27

Perpendicular sliding compact bookcases.

Fig. 28   *Sliding compact cases movable by hand, of the "Hand-Compactus" type.*

principal pioneering value of perpendicular sliding bookcases lies in the fact that they showed how the former frontal passages could be utilized during operations without a decrease in the higher compactness achieved in basic (closed) position; they therefore contributed to a permanently increased capacity of storage areas.

New arrangements of independent perpendicular sliding compact equipment called "Stormor" were made by the English firm J. Glover and Sons. In these independent perpendicular sliding case installations, the cases were placed tightly next to each other by the method proposed by Gladstone, and formed in this way a compact unit uninterrupted by frontal passages. The bookcases did not slide parallel into side passages, but perpendicularly into the space which was taken up in the basic closed position by the neighboring bookcase. A temporary passage was produced by the movement of neighboring bookcases into the reserved passage at the end of the whole row of bookcases which formed the composite compact unit. By a reverse movement, the whole system

Fig. 29

Perpendicular sliding bookcases installed in a basement room, [Compactus equipment in the City and University Library of Bern, Switzerland.]

was brought back into the basic (closed) position or into a newly required position with another temporarily created frontal passage. Instead of frontal passages between each pair of cases, it was thus sufficient to have just one open area which had the dimensions of the width of one bookcase (or a maximum width of 80 to 100 cm.). Instead of the abnormally wide side passage (necessary with parallel sliding cases) it was sufficient to have connecting communications of a minimum standard width.

This arrangement of independent perpendicular sliding bookcases brought about a capacity increase of approximately 40 percent with the use of two paired 1-meter bookcases to a range. After the improvements which were achieved in the "Stormor" products around the year 1936 by a triple and eventually by a quadruple joining of the original compact bookcase 1-meter units, the capacity was increased to 93 or 95 percent. The ratio of

Fig. 30   *Perpendicular sliding bookcases by "Compactus."*

equipment area to passage area, which in standard storage arrangement with stationary bookcases usually amounts to 30:70 or 35:65, was improved to 64:36.

The new design, however, had the disadvantage that considerable physical force was necessary to move a complete compact bookcase section composed of a large number of units. A new composite section of compact bookcases filled with collections might represent a load weighing about two tons.

Movable storage racks were in the meantime utilized in various places including some industrial establishments. One example is the "Foulkes Mobile Storage System," with basic elements similar to the library equipment of the newer types.

The "Stormor" equipment, which was moved by hand, was improved by a patent granted to the Zurich engineer Hans Ingold. In 1947 the English firm J. Glover and Sons and the Swiss firm H. Ingold began to manufacture this new equipment which became generally known as the "Compactus-Ingold System."

Perpendicular sliding compact bookcases of this system quickly found wide application in the next few years, not only in

Fig. 31   *Storage equipped with stationary bookcases at the upper level and perpendicular sliding compact cases at the lower level (Bureau International du Travail [ILO]—Geneva).*

Britain and Switzerland, but also in Sweden, Germany, France, and other countries. They are presently produced under license by several manufacturers in various models and types as either fully automatic, semi-automatic, or manually operated.[4]

Ingold's success was based not only on the correct selection of a system having the best chance for utilization, but also on his being able to master the basic problems of compact equipment with superior techniques of design and manufacture. He was not, of course, satisfied with his initial success and has improved the original design several times, as attested by the fact that he has been granted five additional patents.[5]

These products represent considerable progress, but do not exhaust all the possibilities for further improvements. Without doubt, these improvements will consist not only of technical improvements in compact storage equipment, but also in our present concepts of the construction and organization of storage space, as was pointed out in the proposals of the Soviet architects G. V. Meyendorf and F. N. Pashchenko published in the year 1956. [This is a reference to the article by Pashchenko and Meyendorf listed in the Bibliography—Editor.]

Before we deal with new improvements, let us get acquainted in as much detail as possible with the design by H. Ingold and the products of the "Compactus-Ingold System," and possibly with the newest products of a similar type which have already found various applications abroad.

VII   The "Compactus-Ingold System" equipment is made in three types. The first two, the original "fully automatic" and the improved "semi-automatic," are powered by electricity. The third type, "Hand-Compactus," is moved by hand. The first two types are composed of a number of movable bookcases and one stationary case which houses the motor. The third type consists exclusively of movable cases.

The "Hand-Compactus" equipment is structurally very simple and can be installed in any room since it does not require special preparation of the floor space or special installations. The cases slide on rails on a base which is transportable and can be installed on any floor. In appearance the equipment is similar to office cabinets and is suitable for offices and other nonlibrary installations, as well as for libraries.

The following description and pictures of the fully and semi-automatic type are from Stromeyer, supplemented with some data from articles by F. N. Pashchenko, H. Strahm, F. J. Hill, and L. Kaiser.[6]

The following numbers in parentheses refer to those shown in Fig. 32 which is reprinted from Stromeyer.

Several rails (12, 13) are installed on a concrete floor which must be constructed so as to eliminate future uneven settling. Their number depends on the expected load and on the size of the installation. Two rails (2 and 12) are required in most cases for the undercarriage wheels which run on ball-bearings and another two rails for the towing gear (13, 13a) which will be described later. Instead of U-shaped rails, 15 mm. flat irons are now being used. The undercarriage consists of a braced steel frame structure with a minimum of four ball-bearing wheels (11) at the bottom. The wheels enable the bookcase to move on the rails in the direction parallel to its side panels (perpendicular to the length of the shelves). A double-faced bookcase (10) is erected on this movable undercarriage. The bookcase consists of a central wall which forms the back for

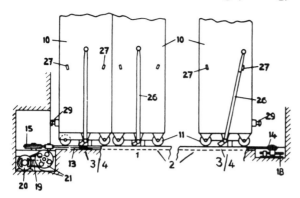

Fig. 32

Diagram of the Ingold system of sliding bookcases.

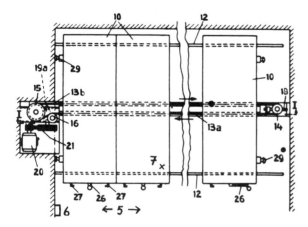

each of the two faces, and full side walls or partitions to which the shelves are fastened. The walls and the upper frame fillers are made of nonburning materials (called "Pavatex" in Switzerland and "Novopan" in East Germany). Steel sheets are used in Sweden, the Soviet Union, and by the West German company, Otto Kind. The shelves have U-shaped metal frames; the loading surface is made of wood—a board 20 mm. thick. The shelves are easily adjustable to different heights (from 10 to 15 mm.).

The change in the position of the sliding bookcases in order to open access to the collections is made by an electric motor. A small motor is sufficient. Hill mentions a ¼ hp. motor; H. Strahm, a three-phase ¾ hp. motor. The latter size is also mentioned by R. Stromeyer, who adds that a ¾ hp. motor serves an installation consisting of 10 to 20 double-faced bookcases. It is obvious that

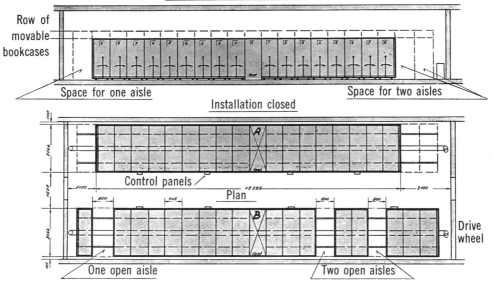

Fig. 33   *Organization of the Ingold system of sliding bookcases.*

the power required depends on the number of units to be served. The motor (20) is placed in the lower part of the stationary case.

The electrical energy is converted into mechanical energy in several ways:

(a) Pull cable equipment

The bookcases are moved with the help of steel cables (13a) when a lever (26) is pressed on one of the bookcases in the direction of the required movement. The lever has a stop (27) on its right and left sides. A continuous steel cable driven by electricity in the floor between the rails is driven by two driving wheels or sprockets (14, 15, 18). Two sliding catches or clamps in the undercarriage latch onto the cable when the lever is pressed. A proper movement of the lever mechanism, with which each bookcase is provided on the side directly and permanently accessible from the connecting passage, causes the clamps in the undercarriage to grip the moving continuous cable in the floor. As the towing cable is subjected to relatively hard wear, and a long cable requires continual adjustment, cables have not been used much lately. (They are still usable in libraries and archives where the maximum load on a cable 14 mm. in diameter would be only about 20 tons, but they are unsuitable for heavier loads, i.e., for the storage of heavier objects than standard library ma-

72

terials.)[7] Experience with other designs has been better, and the argument that the frictional slipping of the cable in the clamps guarantees better safety than in other types of drive is no longer valid. Safety devices in the newest types are designed differently and much more simply. In these types a switch is mounted on the bookcase undercarriage. This switch turns off the motor as soon as it is touched and the bookcases stop immediately.

(b) Toothed driving arrangement

The original fully automatic type used racks built into the floor instead of cables. This design was soon abandoned because the bookcases could not be moved quickly in both directions due to the fact that the rack moved in only one direction at a time. Operations were therefore slowed down because the whole system had to be brought back into the basic closed position after each use. Each operation could be started only with a single master switch key. Stromeyer states that therefore this type is unsuitable for a library; however, the fact that the equipment can be used only by the person who has a special key for the master control switch could make it advantageous for archives.

(c) Chain driven installation

Nearly all the newest designs use a continuous-link chain drive (13a) which moves in a U-shaped rail or in two 45.5 mm. grooves in the concrete. Pins controlled by the lever arrangement fit into the chain link openings. This pulling arrangement passes over the guide rollers or pulleys (14, 15, 18) (the same as in a cable drive, but different from the toothed drive). This ensures that the cases can be opened immediately, in both directions (as marked by arrows in diagrams at 13a), and at any selected place. The disadvantages of the cable system concerning uneven or heavy loads are also eliminated.

Safety devices used in this system can be considered quite sufficient. A timer switch can be set for an interval from 2 to 20, or even up to 40 seconds; the motor is switched off automatically at the end of that interval. A safety button or switch on the separated bookcase must be pressed down for further use. The worker can therefore first see that there is nobody in the opened passage. The use of the safety switch starts the motor again. The desired bookcase then becomes accessible as soon as the lever is moved in the direction of the previously opened temporary passage.

The bookcases are made to order in various sizes. This is advantageous because the dimensions of the equipment can be adjusted to the dimensions of the storage area. The shelves are

Fig. 34

*Installation
of a section of
undercarriages for
Compactus shelving
of Swedish
manufacture.*

22 to 25 cm. deep. The center-to-center distance in closed position is 46 to 52 cm. This is the distance shown between the individual levers (26) when the ranges are closed. All shelves in one bookcase must be of the same width; however, the collections can be stored by size and economical methods of stacking can be applied.[8]

The length of the bookcase ranges can be chosen rather freely. A length of 5 to 6 meters seems most suitable because the equipment can then be used without difficulty should the need arise to move the cases manually. With larger dimensions or exceptionally high loads, two link chain drives are built in parallel to each other, as was done, for example, at the Bayer Dyeworks in Leverkusen [Germany].

Photographs of Swedish "Compactus" products show that their undercarriages are assembled separately. The most widely

Fig. 35

Mounting of the Swedish Compactus cases on the undercarriages.

used undercarriage arrangement in this system is built for 4 or 6 sections of double-faced bookcases. One operational passage is sufficient for 4 to 6 sections of bookcases, each containing from 10 to 15 cases (a total of 40 to 90 bookcases), or double that number if the passage is in the center. The method used to assemble the bookcases themselves is clear from the photographs shown in Figs. 34 and 35.

Let us point out a few more details that should be noted. In determining the bookcase dimensions, it should be kept in mind that the lowest shelf will be 10 to 20 cm. above the surface of the concrete floor. With a new floor installed, the height of the room will be reduced by the necessary concrete base. The height of the equipment is also affected by the requirements of illumination. R. Stromeyer states that a single row of perpendicular fluorescent light fixtures was sufficient in the storage areas studied by him for this purpose, as long as the depth of the bookcase ranges did not exceed 5 to 6 meters. Additional lighting may be installed along operational passages.

Passages of the minimum standard width are sufficient.

The bookcases are always arranged to be accessible only from the central passage. At one end of the range of cases is a wall, and the distance of the last cases from the wall is from 10 to 20 cm. If there are windows in this wall, they should not open on the bookcases. For safety reasons, the area behind the cases should not be used when the system is in operation.

A minimum area 46 to 52 cm. wide [the distance "on centers" between cases] in which to move cases is necessary at one or at both ends of the section of bookcases, depending on the number of movable cases in the section (12 to 20 double-faced bookcases). However, in practice a 70 to 80 cm. dimension is more realistic for operational purposes.

R. Stromeyer states that no equipment repairs had been necessary as yet in the libraries which he visited in 1958.

Either the whole installation or each individual bookcase may be locked; thus the collections are protected against misuse, an important consideration for valuable or rare collections. The bookcases in basic (closed) position are fitted with rubber bumpers or baffles (which also have a sealing function), and overhanging frame members.

Storage, maintenance and cleaning costs are reduced in proportion to the reduced storage area. Operational costs are increased, of course, by the additional use of electricity, which, however, is relatively insignificant.

The electric motor can be placed either in the wall behind the last movable case or in the middle of the bookcase section (which is more common). Two electric motors can be installed in one stationary case; then 20 to 38 movable double-faced bookcases can be placed between two stationary cases, and all movable cases can slide simultaneously (a complete section of up to 37 double-faced movable bookcases!). These properties of "Compactus-Ingold System" shelving represent very important advantages and have important economic consequences, especially in certain kinds of storage areas.

Certain building and technical conditions must be observed in the construction and installation of this compact system. A perfectly level floor surface is necessary. In most installations concrete floors are used. The required load-bearing capacity is 500 to 1400 kg. per square meter of floor space. (The pressure on a wheel is about 430 kg.) This requirement is quite substantial; consequently the system has been installed mostly in basement rooms up to the present time. A multi-story storage building requires a module in which the load-bearing piers and vertical supports are spaced to correspond to the most efficient arrangement of the equipment and to operational needs. R. Stromeyer states than an area 30 by 4 meters with an expected load of 1350 kg. per square meter requires a floor 0.20 meters thick; an area 7.80 by 11 meters requires a floor 0.30 meters thick.

The protection of collections in the "Compactus-Ingold System" will be examined later in our comparative study of all compact systems, as the advantages and disadvantages in details are not decisive enough to warrant a separate discussion here.

On the other hand, there are some important questions of an operational nature. We will note here at least those which were mentioned by Stromeyer.

The motor, started with a switch (6), does not require a warm-up period; the levers (26) which are used to move one or more sliding cases can be used immediately when the motor is turned on. The action of the motor can be preset to 2, 20, or 40 seconds. If it is set to 20 seconds, books can be removed from an average of two different aisles before the section is closed again by the action of the motor. The time required for this operation is lessened by the shortened communications due to the compact placement of one bookcase against another. The following savings in communications are obtained in an installation composed of 18 double-faced ranges 50 cm. wide [center-to-center distance] and two single-faced stationary wall cases 25 cm. wide: the distance between the fortieth range and the first one in an open position of the compact system is 10.05 meters (18 × 0.50 meters + 0.25 meters + 0.80 meters [for the aisle]). A system of stationary cases with a center-to-center distance of 1.30 meters would require 24.5 meters. The saving is therefore at least 58.9 percent. The savings in communication distances, and therefore in operational time, increase with the size of the compact system.

We have not included anything on equipment and construction costs for two reasons. First, we will do that later in an economical analysis based on data available from various sources abroad. Second, since compact bookcases are not yet being manufactured in Czechoslovakia, we have no reliable figures of our own, and the data from abroad would be only theoretical.[9]

We mentioned previously that shelving is produced under the Ingold patent not only in Switzerland, but also in Britain, Sweden,

Germany, and France. The French products made by the firm F.A.M.A.C. [Fabrique Alsacienne de Matériel et d'Articles de Classement] come in two types, a fully automatic and a semi-automatic type.

Among the French products of perpendicular sliding compact bookcases, the suspension-type cases of the NASH and BDR type should also be mentioned. The products by NASH [Nord et Alpes-Schwartz-Haumont] are provided with pneumatic equipment. The suspension structure is erected above the system of bookcases. The BDR products (made by Baudet Donon Roussel) have a similar design; they are either automatic (using compressed air), or manual. The size of the case units is 3 to 4 meters.[10]

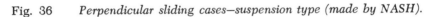

Fig. 36   *Perpendicular sliding cases—suspension type (made by NASH).*

Fig. 37

*Perpendicular
sliding cases
—suspension type
(made by BDR).*

The sides of these French cases are easily adaptable for a three-sided placement of books because the levers take up a minimum of space (they can be seen on the lower part of the NASH cases pictured in Fig. 36, and on the center part of the BDR cases shown in Fig. 37).

VIII The descriptions of the products mentioned above and other makes of this type are accurate as far as the main features are concerned. The details of individual makes differ, of course, not only among the different trademarks, but even within the same trademark when their construction is adapted for local conditions or for the special requirements of individual libraries, archives, and other users who plan to install such equipment in existing storage areas. The adaptations are often quite ingenious, and in many cases are improvements on the original design. They are a proof that the creative cooperation of technicians, librarians, and other users may lead to the design of new and more effective types. It is interesting to note that sometimes more than one type of compact shelving system can be found in a single work area.

In our opinion this mixing of equipment types will be common in most libraries in the future because various types of collections and varing local conditions require the selection of different equipment to meet specific needs. The mixture found at present is caused mainly by the search for the best type of equipment and the gradual introduction of new types on the basis of previous experience. An example is the Bureau International du Travail [ILO] in Geneva, where the first compact bookcases were installed in 1930, and others after World War II.[11] A similar situation exists in Sweden, where the first compact bookcases (of English make) were introduced in the archives of the Foreign Office through the initiative of its director Dr. Uno Willers after World War II. Within a few years the use of compact storage cases and also their production had expanded in Sweden to such a degree that in the opinion of the Soviet specialist, the architect F. N. Pashchenko, the current Swedish products are among the best in the world.[12] The Swedish firm AB Electrolux at Säffle has gained valuable experience, which should be useful here in Czechoslovakia. This firm produces not only the automatic types, but has also begun production of an improved version of manually operated equipment, which has become very popular.[13] F. N. Pashchenko, who in 1939 had designed the first compact storage warehouse in the Soviet Union, recently made a study of this equipment while in Sweden; in his opinion a similar type of equipment will find wide application in Soviet libraries and archives.

IX   Compact bookcases are not a new item in the Soviet Union. The first compact warehouse was designed in 1939 by architect F. N. Paschenko for the Library of the USSR Academy of Sciences in Moscow.[14] In 1948 the architect K. Gutin, in consultation with F. N. Pashchenko, designed a compact storage

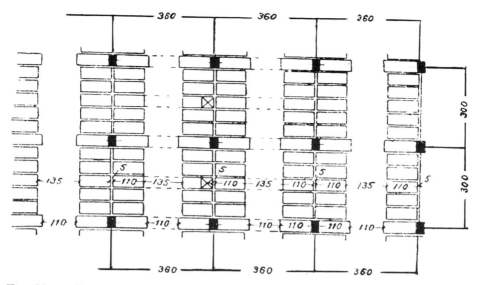

Fig. 38   *Diagrammatic plan of a warehouse section equipped with parallel sliding compact cases (new building of The Library of the Academy of Sciences of The USSR [1939]).*

area for the Karelian ASSR (Autonomous Soviet Socialist Republic) State Public Library in Petrozavodsk. Since that time compact bookcases can be found in all new building projects for large Soviet libraries.[15] The matter of compact shelving and storage is very popular in the Soviet Union; during my visit in 1958 there was not a single discussion in which Soviet librarians and architects would not discuss very knowledgeably the problems of such equipment. They are convinced that it will be widely used. The Soviet Union devotes special care to the theoretical study of compact storage problems and to experimental research. The work of V. A. Marin with the "Russian Collection" of the Saltykov-Shchedrin Library in Leningrad was mentioned in the description of drawer-type compact shelving in Part III. The work of F. N. Pashchenko, G. V. Meyendorf, and A. Sabitov should also be mentioned. Many other workers are studying the same problems, but have not published the results of their studies as yet. The present systems of compact shelving are being subjected to a great deal of critical examination in the Soviet Union. Soviet products, which have not yet entered the stage of mass production, will without doubt find extensive application when the best type is standardized, or when various types are perfected for specific conditions in libraries, archives, and similar places.

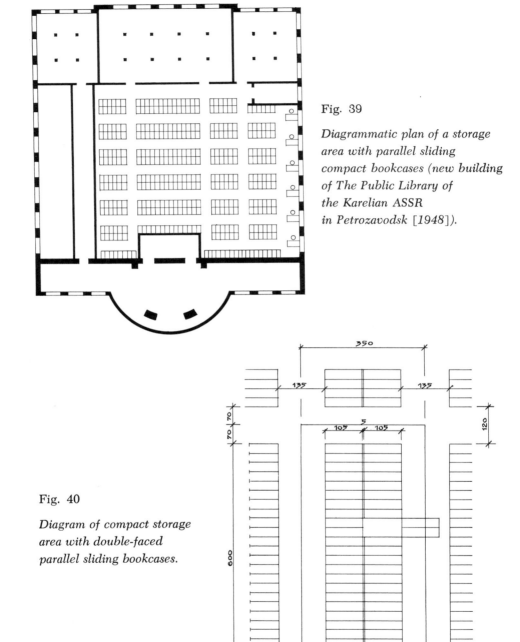

Fig. 39

*Diagrammatic plan of a storage
area with parallel sliding
compact bookcases (new building
of The Public Library of
the Karelian ASSR
in Petrozavodsk [1948]).*

Fig. 40

*Diagram of compact storage
area with double-faced
parallel sliding bookcases.*

But it is still important at least to become acquainted with the prototype of the perpendicular sliding compact bookcase by G. V. Meyendorf installed in the Lenin Library and with the equipment designed by A. Sabitov which has been installed in the State Historical Library in Moscow.

The test model made under the direction of G. V. Meyendorf for the Lenin Library in Moscow is a double-faced perpendicular sliding compact bookcase, 100 cm. long, made of metal. It is equipped with four wheels fastened to the base. The steel frame structure is braced by an inside frame, which at the same time serves as supporting standards for the shelves. The stability of the case is further increased by four steel bands on the outside

Fig. 41

*Model of a bookcase unit
designed by the architect
G. V. Meyendorf.*

of the bookcase sides which are placed at the level of the third shelf from the bottom and the second shelf from the top. The shelves are adjustable and can be set at 10 mm. intervals. According to the statement by the designer, the metal shelves will later be replaced by shelves made of synthetic materials. A new Soviet material which has already proved successful in tests is being considered; the core is made of a light foam material, "penoplast," and the surface of "steklospon" [author's transliterations], which is known for durability, and its resistance to moisture, fire, pressure, abrasion, etc. An experimental shelf weighs about 500 grams.

The cases which have been in operation for several years in the State Historical Library in Moscow are installed in an old building with a warehouse area of 196 square meters [see Fig. 42]. The warehouse space for compact storage was created by the

Fig. 42

Soviet sliding shelves
—perpendicular sliding type
(State Historical Library,
Moscow).

adaptation of the first and second floors with the help of load-bearing iron lintels.

The basic compact unit, according to the technical description by A. Sabitov attached to the shop drawings donated to Dr. J. Těšitel of the University of Chemical Technology in Pardubice, Czechoslovakia, by the State Historical Library in Moscow, is a double-faced cabinet-type bookcase 1910 by 1965 by 480 mm. (These dimensions differ slightly from those given in the article by E. Lesyuk and A. Sabitov [listed in the Bibliography]. The dimensions shown in that article are 1850 by 1970 by 475 mm.)

Angle iron (20 by 20 by 2 mm.) with diagonal bracing (20 by 2 by 4 mm.) was used in the frame construction. The grooving for shelves, which can be set in 10 mm. steps, has dimensions of 10 by 20 mm. The bookcase walls and the partition in the center are made of sheet steel 1 mm. thick. The outer edge flanges are made of rubber to reduce the impact in closing the section and to ensure a tight fit of the bookcase section in the closed position. The adjustable shelves are made of sheet steel (1 mm.) and are provided with catches (2 mm. sheet steel). The total weight of one shelf is 2.2 kg. The total weight of the case with 20 to 28 shelves averages 100 kg. This weight can be substantially reduced if the metal shelves are replaced by shelves made of synthetic materials (these shelves would weigh about 500 grams), and if the steel panels are replaced by panels made of synthetic materials.

The case is equipped with an iron undercarriage which has two axles (24 mm. in diameter) for four wheels (150 mm. in diameter) with ball-bearings (No. 205). A chain gear is used; the toothed wheels have different diameters and a different number of teeth, selected in a ratio which makes possible manual control with a minimum of effort. The equipment is moved by a revolving wheel 400 mm. in diameter, situated in the middle section of the side which faces the connecting passage. The gear system (chain and gears) is protected by the side panel of the case, but the revolving wheel is on the outside, and directly accessible from the passage. Total weight of the undercarriage, including the gear and the running structure, is about 85 kg. The complete bookcase unit including shelves, but without books, weighs about 185 kg. This means that equipment weighing 90 to 95 kg. provides 12 to 14 meters of loading surface. This can be improved by replacing metal parts with synthetic materials.

The compact bookcase sections are organized in systems of twelve of the units described above. The cases move on a metal track (20 by 20 mm.). Movements to any required distance are made by the manual turning of the wheel. The manipulation is quite simple, and I have verified that it does not require any special exertion. According to the employees, who are mostly women, and with whom I discussed in detail the advantages and disadvantages of the system, its operation is not demanding. Work safety is also well ensured. The system achieved a threefold increase in the capacity of the original warehouse space, and in addition it increased the operational effectiveness by shortened communications and by the removal of the high stationary cases which required steps, ladders, etc. The only item of this prototype unsatisfactory to the experts is its surface finish.

X   In conclusion, let us summarize at least briefly the most important conclusions relating not only to parallel and perpendicular sliding compact shelves, but also to the other systems of compact storage, in the light of their possible application for libraries and other storage areas in Czechoslovakia.

(a) Perpendicular sliding compact bookcases should be given preference in the production of storage equipment, because of their superior effectiveness and all-around range of application.

One- and 2-meter manual units, and automatic units with 4- and 6-meter undercarriages should be considered.

(b) In order to obtain the maximum utilization of compact storage areas, it will be necessary to produce parallel sliding compact cases and drawer-type compact shelving to be used as complementary equipment.

In order to increase the capacity of drawer-type cases in a combined arrangement with perpendicular sliding compact bookcases, a design must be found which would enlarge the drawer length to from 270 to 275 cm. and still keep the drawers at a permanently horizontal level at any open position and with any load.

For combined systems of perpendicular and parallel sliding cases, the design of parallel sliding cases must be improved to make possible the use of manually operated 2-meter units without rails or suspension devices, and the construction of such units 270 to 275 cm. long.

(c) Stationary cases will remain in use and their production must continue, but with improved designs which make possible both their independent use and their employment in combined units and systems, with particular emphasis on their possible use in the remodeling of storage areas and reading areas in public libraries.

(d) Revolving compact shelves are applicable in special circumstances. It will be sufficient to begin the production of prototypes and of specific, individual orders.

(e) Two lines of improvement are necessary for full utilization of compact shelving: an improvement in design to increase its capacity, and an increase in the number of volumes accessible without auxiliary operations.

(f) The stability of collections placed in movable cases and on movable shelves must be ensured to at least the level common to collections stored in stationary cases of traditional types in order to ensure their maximum protection.

(g) New projects for buildings and storage areas must meet the construction requirements necessary for compact storage. Typical plans should be prepared for well organized compact storage areas to be used in different types of libraries using various types of compact storage shelves both in independent and combined groupings.

PART FIVE

New Ways of Economical Organization of Storage Space in the USSR and Czechoslovakia

I   The theoretical work of Soviet specialists in the field of perpendicular sliding compact cases is concerned with the problem of the maximum utilization of storage areas in both old and newly planned buildings.

Two plans for storage space remodeling are proposed for old buildings by the architects F. N. Pashchenko and G. V. Meyendorf.[16]

In the first plan they recommend the addition of single-faced parallel sliding bookcases along one side of a range of stationary shelves in old warehouses having double-faced cases of the traditional type with a center-to-center distance of 140 to 145 cm., i.e., with frontal passages at least 95 cm. wide. The number of supplementary sliding units to be installed in the frontal passage should correspond to the number of original stationary units less one. This means that the range of sliding units is 100 cm. shorter than the stationary range. This reduction is necessary to make possible access to the collections on the stationary shelves, which are covered by the newly installed movable bookcases. Access to a stationary shelf is obtained by sliding a movable case into the area reserved at the beginning or end of each row of movable cases and then, if necessary, successively sliding the other movable cases until the desired stationary shelf section is uncovered. To make this concept clear we have added a diagram [Fig. 43] showing ranges consisting of six 1-meter sections of double-faced stationary cases, supplemented by five 1-meter sections of movable single-faced cases placed along only one side of the stationary ranges. It is evident from this diagram that out of the 17 one-meter sections now in each range, only 12 are directly accessible (which is the same number which were accessible in

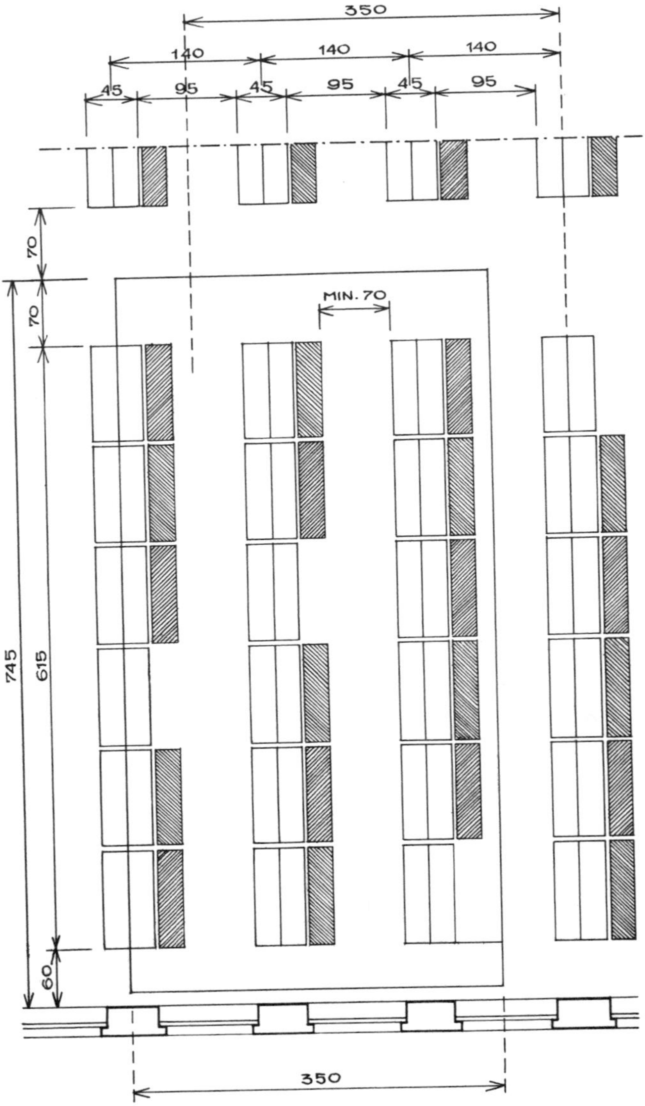

Fig. 43

*Storage area
with unnecessarily wide
aisles, supplemented with
single-faced parallel
sliding cases on one side
of original passages.*

the original ranges of stationary cases), while five sections are accessible only after the movement of the sliding cases stationed in front of them. The capacity of the remodeled storage area is increased by 26 to 28 percent. The new frontal passages will still have the required standard width (70 to 75 cm.).

In the second plan, designed for old warehouses with double-faced cases of the traditional type having a center-to-center distance of 170 cm., i.e., with frontal passages at least 115 cm. wide,

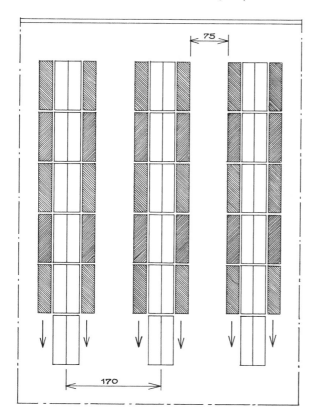

Fig. 44

Storage area
with unnecessarily wide
aisles, supplemented with
single-faced parallel
sliding cases on both sides
of original passages.

the architects recommend the addition of single-faced parallel sliding cases along both sides of the stationary ranges [Fig. 44]. The supplementary sliding cases are installed in the original frontal passages in the same manner as in the previous plan and their method of operation is also the same. Storage capacity is increased in this plan by 29 to 33 percent. The new frontal passages are still about 75 cm. wide.

In the first plan 1.26 square meters of floor space are required for 14 meters of loading surface; in the second plan 1.20 square meters are necessary. In both plans the number of directly accessible shelf sections is the same as it was in the original stationary storage arrangement.

This type of reconstruction is advantageous for several reasons. The original stationary bookcases can be used without adaptation and no expenses are incurred in moving them from their original position. In some libraries it is not even

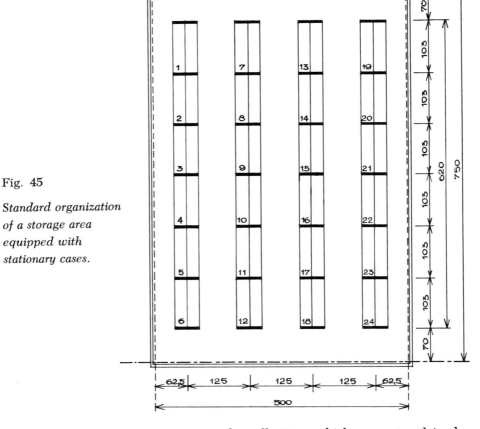

Fig. 45

Standard organization of a storage area equipped with stationary cases.

necessary to rearrange the collections which were stored in the stationary bookcases. Therefore the installation costs are minimal if the load-bearing properties of the floor are sufficient. The sliding movement is done manually and is not difficult even with 5-meter sliding sections.

When compared with the installation in the old storage areas of the British Museum, which we mentioned in Part Four in our description of the earliest installations of parallel sliding compact bookcases, we can see that the Soviet specialists have made a substantial improvement with this design. The Iron Library of the British Museum storage had in some instances a 4:1 and in others a 2:1 ratio of stationary bookcases to movable cases while here a much more desirable ratio of 12:5 or 12:10 has been obtained.

F. N. Pashchenko states that the plan using sliding cases placed along both sides of stationary shelves is suitable for the old storage area of the Lenin Library, which was built toward

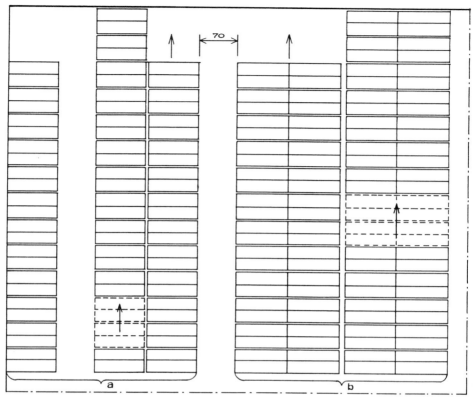

Fig. 46   *Storage area proposed by G. V. Meyendorf (2-meter perpendicular sliding bookcases).*

the end of the 19th century. Using this plan, the capacity of this so-called iron warehouse with its 115 cm. wide passages would be increased by 80 to 83 percent.

(In this connection it should be mentioned, at least marginally, that revolving compact shelves could also be employed in storage areas with passages 95 or 115 cm. wide—the double-wing type in the former and the single-wing type in the latter. It would be instructive to investigate the comparative capacity, costs, and operating conditions both in general terms and in the actual situation of the storage area of the Lenin Library and of the Library of the National Museum in Prague where a similar situation needs to be solved under conditions [sufficient load-bearing strength of floor areas, solid bookcase structure] which are particularly suitable for revolving shelves.)

The architects F. N. Pashchenko and G. V. Meyendorf have also proposed several designs for storage areas in new Soviet library buildings.

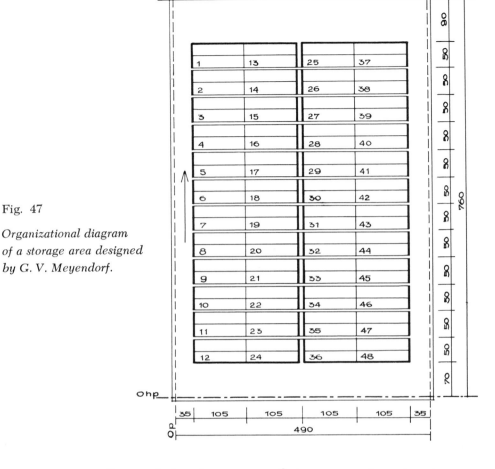

Fig. 47

Organizational diagram
of a storage area designed
by G. V. Meyendorf.

In one design they propose that a passage in a storage area equipped with parallel sliding compact cases should always be utilized on both sides, i.e., for two ranges of parallel sliding cases. A compact storage area of this type using double-faced parallel sliding cases in groups of 24 units can achieve nearly 1.5 times increased capacity [see Fig. 46]. The floor space necessary for 14 meters of shelf would be reduced to 1.06 square meters.

Even more substantial saving in floor space is achieved in the design by G. V. Meyendorf for a storage area equipped with perpendicular sliding compact cases. The application of his previously described 2-meter compact cases [see Part Four] reduces the floor area necessary for 14 meters of shelf to a mere 0.78 square meters.[17]

This means that a saving of one-half of the total storage area is achieved in comparison with the floor space required for 14

94

meters of shelf in a storage installation of the traditional type (0.78 square meters compared to 1.56 square meters).

This design doubles the loading surface capacity in comparison with the manually operated 1-meter perpendicular sliding bookcase in the Compactus type products of Swiss or English manufacture. The experience of the State Historical Library in Moscow shows that manual operation of a 2-meter bookcase is not difficult; and, of course, the Soviet authors also count on future mechanization with pneumatic equipment or electric motors.

When these designs are compared with the Swedish system of 4- to 6-meter sections of perpendicular sliding cases, it is necessary to keep in mind that the Ingold type bookcases are most suitable for narrow storage areas (170 to 270 cm. wide), Meyendorf's cases are most suitable in storage areas 270 cm. or 470 cm. wide, and the Swedish Compactus bookcases are only suitable in large storage areas (from 470 to 670 or 870, or possibly 1270, cm. wide).

II Although compact shelving has not yet been used in Czechoslovakia, it has been the subject of studies for several years. After the publication of the 1956 article by Pashchenko and Meyendorf [see Bibliography], the questions of economy in storage areas and the standardization of equipment for libraries were included in the work plans of the Section for Library Technique and Work Organization of the Central Library Council of Czechoslovakia. The first results appeared in the winter of 1957-58 in the form of supplementary proposals for the Soviet design for a storage area organized by means of parallel and perpendicular sliding compact bookcases. These proposals were accepted even before the date of their publication in 1958.[18] They were published in Soviet professional literature in 1959.[19]

The substance of the supplementary proposals is as follows:

1. For a combined system of parallel sliding cases.

In a compact storage area originally equipped with double-faced parallel sliding bookcases, it is proposed that such equipment should be supplemented with single-faced parallel sliding bookcases as follows:

(a) Where the side passages are 110 cm. wide (the usual minimum passage width in this type of compact system), it is proposed that one row of single-faced parallel sliding cases be installed in each passage along the total length of each section, except for a 100 cm. space to be left at the end of the range.

The original surplus width of permanent aisles is reduced in this system to 85 cm., which is still more than the prescribed standard width. [See Variation a, Fig. 48.]

(b) Where the original side passages are 130 to 135 cm. wide (which is the case with most foreign products of this type, and which is also the width assumed by F. N. Pashchenko and G. V. Meyendorf), it is proposed that *two* rows of single-faced parallel sliding cases be installed in each passage along the total length of each section (one row along each side of the passage with a 100 cm. space left at the end). The original surplus width of the permanent passages is reduced in this system to 80 or 85 cm., which is again still more than the prescribed standard width. [See Variation b, Fig. 49.]

The introduction of this system would not cause greater operational difficulty than those described by Soviet authors for a combined system of movable and stationary cases, nor would it require more mechanization or increased construction costs.

Fig. 48

Combined system of parallel sliding bookcases. Variation a. (Designed by D. Gawrecki.)

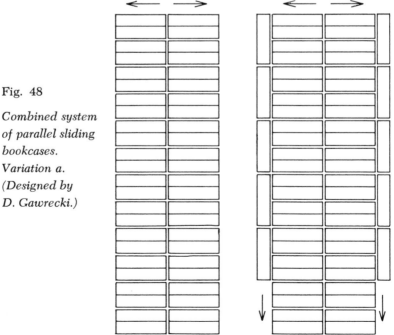

The unused area of surplus passages would be reduced by nearly 20 percent in Variation a, and by more than 30 percent in Variation b.

2. For a combined system of perpendicular sliding cases and stationary cases of the traditional type.

In a compact storage area originally equipped with perpendicular sliding cases, it is proposed that the capacity be increased by using stationary cases in the following way:

Stationary double-faced cases are to be built along the entire length of this passage between the ranges of the perpendicular sliding compact bookcases to form the central portion of the combined system of bookcases. The length of the stationary bookcase row overlaps the length of the sliding case sections by the dimension of the area reserved for the movement of the sliding bookcases. [See Fig. 50.]

The access to a stationary case is made possible by sliding away the proper movable bookcase. No change in the width of the remaining passages is necessary.

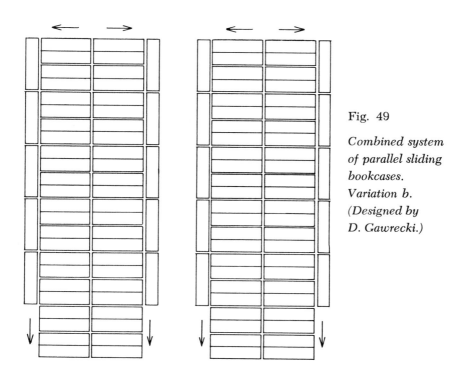

Fig. 49

Combined system of parallel sliding bookcases. Variation b. (Designed by D. Gawrecki.)

Compact Library Shelving

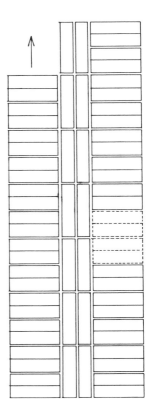

Fig. 50

Combined system of perpendicular sliding bookcases and stationary cases. (Designed by D. Gawrecki.)

Increased capacity is obtained without a demand on new passages. Only 0.45 square meters of floor space are needed to gain an extra 14 meters of loading surface.

This method can be applied to all types of perpendicular sliding compact bookcases. The degree of effectiveness depends on the length of the sliding bookcases. With 1-meter compact cases, the capacity of the equipment would be increased by 49 meters of new loading surface for each 168 meters of original loading surface.

3. For a combined system of cases which have both a perpendicular and parallel sliding movement and stationary shelving of the traditional type.

The compact storage of the Meyendorf system is organized in such a way that one main passage is made sufficient for the whole storage area, and stationary single-faced cases are used as supplementary equipment along the walls. This design assumes that the access to the individual bookcases is obtained by step-by-step parallel and perpendicular movements of the movable cases. [See Fig. 51.]

For example, access to the movable bookcases $6d_4$ and $6d_5$ in the diagram can be gained as follows: slide cases 1 through 5 of sections d_4 and d_5 in a perpendicular direction into the passage marked a. A temporary aisle has now been formed in front of cases $6d_4$ and $6d_5$, and access to them may be gained from the passage marked b. Access to the cases in section d_6 can be gained by first moving as many cases in sections d_4 and d_5 as necessary in a parallel direction into passage b, thus creating a temporary aisle between sections d_5 and d_6, and then moving the necessary number of cases in section d_6 in a perpendicular direction into passage a. Access to the cases in the range marked c_2 may be gained by various combinations of parallel and perpendicular movements of the cases in sections d_4, d_5, and d_6.

Access to individual cases on the other side of passage b (sections d_1, d_2, d_3, and range c_1) can be gained in the same manner.

The collections in the ranges c_3 and c_4 are, of course, directly accessible from passage a, as are cases $1d_1$ through $1d_6$ and the first cases in ranges c_1 and c_2.

This method would increase the storage capacity of an area to its maximum. The size of the area would be limited only by

Fig. 51

Diagram of
a compact
storage area.
(Designed by
D. Gawrecki.)

a — *Passage including area for the movement of sliding bookcases (100 to 170 cm. wide).*
b — *Central passage (temporary side passage 70 cm. wide).*
c — *Single-faced stationary cases of the traditional type.*
d — *Movable cases (200 cm. long).*

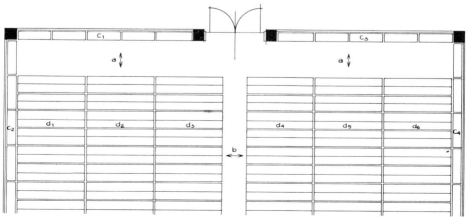

an acceptable construction module and the proper technical conditions.

The only disadvantages lie in the double operation required for the parallel and perpendicular movement of bookcases and in the more complicated construction of the bookcases themselves.

I had assumed originally that a combined suspension and floor rail system would be necessary for such an application; however, this disadvantage has been eliminated by a Swedish system [AB Electrolux, Säffle] of 4- to 6-meter undercarriages for perpendicular sliding compact bookcases, which was unknown to me at the time I worked on the above proposal. The Swedish arrangement makes expensive suspended installations unnecessary, and designs passage b as a permanent aisle. It represents a very advantageous solution from both the operational and the construction points of view.

However, I still consider the organization of storage space proposed above as a starting point for achieving maximum compactness in large storage areas.

III   Our work in Czechoslovakia in the field of compact storage has developed in roughly the following steps: A list of professional literature was prepared, and articles, books and manufacturers' literature were obtained from abroad. Then a systematic and detailed study of new types of shelving and the economical organization of storage space was undertaken, and increased cooperation and exchange of knowledge with specialists abroad was started. In 1959 and 1960 several Czechoslovak libraries started planning to equip their storage areas with compact shelving, and compact storage has been proposed in plans for new buildings.

At the present time we are confronted by the following pressing tasks:

(1) To prepare the reconstruction of two large rooms in the library of the National Museum in Prague for the storage of rare Czech collections.

(2) To make binding decisions on the most suitable application of compact shelving to be used in the complex of the State Library of Czechoslovakia.

(3) To secure compact shelves for the training library of the Chair of Library Science and the Philological Library at Charles

University in Prague, the library of the University of Chemical Technology in Pardubice, and for the planned building of Matica Slovenská in Martin.

(4) To prepare designs for the remodeling of storage areas in several large state science libraries and state archives.

(5) To design prototypes of Czechoslovak products in the field of compact bookcases of various types.

(6) To secure industrial production of Czechoslovak compact shelving of standardized types, which are suitable for various storage applications (libraries, archives, offices, manufacturing plants, etc.).

IV   For the purpose of acquainting the reader with the work being done in the field of compact shelving in Czechoslovakia, we have included a diagram [Fig. 52] and a brief description of a storage area organized for maximum compactness which the author prepared during 1959 and 1960.

[Editor's note: Section IV has been rewritten, and the original drawing has been revised by the author.]

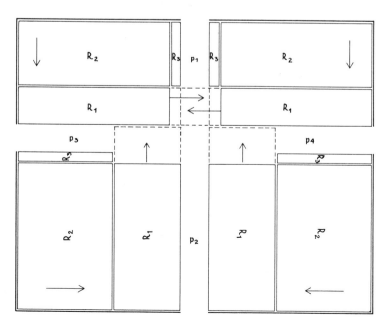

Fig. 52

Diagram of a storage area arranged for maximum compactness. (Designed by D. Gawrecki.)

The diagram shows a storage area (which could possibly be only one of a number of sections in a larger storage area) that can be expanded in all directions according to operational needs or to fit the architectural details of the building in which it is located.

The area shown in the diagram is zoned into a number of sections equipped with stationary cases of the traditional type, perpendicular sliding cases, and either drawer-type or parallel sliding cases. In the diagram the sections equipped with perpendicular sliding cases are marked R_1, the sections equipped with parallel sliding or drawer-type cases are marked R_2, and the sections made up of stationary shelves are marked R_3. The passages or aisles are marked p_1, p_2, p_3, and p_4.

When the sections within the area are in the basic (closed) position, the only directly accessible books (or other stored materials) are those stored on the stationary shelves, those on the shelves along the length of the perpendicular sliding cases facing on aisles p_2, p_3, p_4, and possibly some of those on the narrow ends of these cases, provided that they are constructed in a manner similar to the three-way drawer-type shelves known as "Hamilton Compo Stack."

The books which are not directly accessible in the basic (closed) position of the shelf sections are made accessible by moving the perpendicular sliding cases forward into the aisles. This enables the books on the shelves of the parallel sliding or drawer-type cases to be reached by pulling those shelves out into the temporary aisle created by the movement of the perpendicular sliding cases.

The diagram is, of course, only theoretical. For practical purposes, the use of suitable types of shelving equipment and their arrangement within the storage area is conditioned by the size of the area, by the dimensions of the construction module, by other details of the building construction, and by operational needs.

The most difficult problem in the organization of an area for maximum compactness is the composition and the arrangement of cases in the individual sections of the combined system. It is apparent, for example, that parallel sliding cases placed next to the walls must be of a single-faced construction. Otherwise, the books stored on the shelves of these cases facing the walls would be absolutely inaccessible. When arranging the parallel sliding or drawer-type shelving it is necessary to choose an arrangement which will guarantee that during the operation of the system, all drawers or shelves will be accessible under normal working conditions.

As far as the dimensions of the cases are concerned, the perpendicular sliding cases can be placed on 1- to 6- meter undercarriages. The length of the drawer-type or parallel sliding cases depends on the dimensions of the perpendicular sliding cases and the width of the aisles. For example, the length of the cases in the section marked R_2 in the lower right-hand corner of Figure 52 cannot exceed the length of the perpendicular sliding cases in the adjacent section marked R_1 plus the width of aisle p_2, otherwise it would not be possible to pull them out to their full length. The length of these perpendicular sliding or drawer-type shelves is also limited by their structural strength and by the physical effort required to move them out when they are fully loaded.

The use of the single-faced stationary shelves is supplementary. They can be used in the areas between sections of movable shelves, or at the ends of these sections, or along the walls of the storage area, wherever there is room.

By selecting various types of shelving, it is possible to work out other combined systems designed to achieve maximum compactness, again depending on the function of the system, operational necessities, and the dimensions and architectural layout of the area to be used.

It is assumed that a compact storage area of this type will normally not have windows. Window openings may, however, sometimes be necessary under certain circumstances, and it would be possible to at least partially furnish the area with natural daylight if required.

V   Although we have no tradition in compact storage equipment in Czechoslovakia, it should be mentioned that the idea of compact storage and the economical organization of storage space was investigated more than 35 years ago by a library worker, the engineer Herman Mayerhöfer, a longtime director of the Polytechnic Library (State Technical Library) in Brno.

In the last four years study in this area has been undertaken by the following people besides the author: Eva Vránová (in her unpublished dissertation entitled: "Stavby a architektura knihoven" ["The construction and architecture of libraries"], Department of Library Science, Charles University, Prague, 1956),

Jiří Rys, Dr. J. Těšitel, and R. Pittermann. Systematic work in this field has also been done recently by Jaroslav Drtina and Dr. Jiří Kábrt, who plan to include it in their lectures at the Chair of Library Science at Charles University in Prague. The idea of the practical application of compact shelving in Czechoslovak libraries is supported intensively by the representatives of the Czechoslovak Central Librarian Council, led by the director of the Czechoslovak State Library, Josef Hušek, and by Jaroslav Lipovsky, in charge of the Department of Libraries at the Ministry of Education and Culture. Conditions for the practical application of such equipment are being prepared by the collectives of workers in the Library of the National Musem in Prague under the leadership of Dr. Karel Švehla, the Philosophical Faculty of Charles University, Dr. Josef Navrátil, director of the State Medical Library in Prague, workers of the cooperative firm DEZA, engineers A. Pechánek and Z. Kovařík, the cooperative in Pardubice, and the workers of Matica Slovenská under the director Juraj Paška in Slovakia. Important contributions have come from Dr. Jaroslav Kunc, director of the National Library in Prague, Valentin Pešat, director of the Technical Library in the Klement Gottwald plant of the Vitkovické Iron Works, and many other persons who are following achievements in this field with interest and enthusiasm.

VI   The personnel of the Military Political Academy in Prague have proved in the past few months that at least partial success can be achieved by relatively simple methods. Their example will certainly prompt wide response and will contribute at least a partial solution to the space problem in other libraries until the industrial production of standardized Czechoslovak equipment for compact storage of collections can be begun.

The information about compact storage in Czechoslovak libraries would not be complete without a detailed description of the results achieved in the library of the Military Political Academy. Under the direction of Stanislav Štingl, Librarian Jaroslav Skolek made an "improvement proposal" for the remodeling of stationary double-faced bookcases. This proposal, prepared in December, 1959, led to the first practical application of parallel sliding bookcases in Czechoslovakia.

The bookcases are installed in a former corridor adjacent to the main storage area.

It is interesting to note that the redesign, if we can call it that in this particular case, consists merely of the attachment of movable elements to the base of the stationary bookcase, without any further modification of the original case, without any special undercarriage design, or without adaptation of the storage area or its floor surface.

According to his own statement, Skolek learned about the existence of compact storage shelving only in a general way during his studies of library science prior to 1956. The information gleaned in his study of my article "Pro ekonomické využití skladištních prostorů v knovnách" ("For Economical Usage of Storage Areas in Libraries") [see Bibliography] helped him to design a more effective method for the storage of the collections. Since I published in that article only a reproduction of the parallel sliding bookcases of the Toronto Public Library without a description of the sliding mechanisms, he solved this problem independently. It should be recognized that his solution has the advantage of simplicity and is structurally undemanding.

He used the SKF steerable and fixed wheels [swivel and fixed type casters], which are commonly sold here and used for small carts. The base of a bookcase was equipped with two steerable wheels in front (on the side which moves into the passage when the bookcase is moved) and with two fixed wheels in the back. The combination of steerable and fixed wheels was successful, but the initial experience showed that fixed wheels alone are quite sufficient for parallel sliding bookcases. The SKF wheels are equipped with ball-bearings and solid rubber tires. They are made of quality grey cast iron and have the advantage of easy and quiet movement. The carrying capacity of such wheels ranges from 75 kg. to 250 kg., depending on the type. The steerable wheels (SKF type TJ 4) and the fixed wheels (SKF type TF 4) used in the equipment had a diameter of 100 mm. and a carrying capacity of 125 kg.

The floor of the VPA (Military Political Academy) library in Prague where this equipment was installed is tiled, but in spite of that, the handling of the sliding cases does not cause difficulties, even to female personnel. The direction of the sliding movement is controlled very easily with fixed wheels even with the 14-shelf bookcases fully loaded. Due to the ease of movement, the volumes on partially loaded shelves do not tend to fall out, even though no special supports are used. The total height of the formerly stationary bookcases was increased by approximately 5 cm. According to the computations by Captain Stanislav Štingl, a 35 percent saving of storage space was achieved by this method.

We should also check the suitability of the so-called free-turning SKF wheels which are available here. In my opinion, the free-turning wheels with a diameter of 180 mm., 200 mm., and 225 mm. should be considered for 2-meter parallel sliding bookcases. Larger wheel diameters make possible easier movement of the cases, and a simple, inexpensive construction of 2-meter hand-operated parallel sliding cases will very likely make possible installations of a combined system of parallel and perpendicular sliding bookcases without the use of electric or other power systems. The free-turning wheels are equipped with hubcaps and can be mounted on an axle. These properties are important for the design of perpendicular sliding bookcases. We should test experimentally the possibility of using perpendicular sliding bookcases which move without rails, i.e., in the same manner as parallel sliding bookcases.

The free-turning SKF wheels are well sealed with no leakage of lubrication grease; there is no soiling of the floor or the collections. The bearings are greased once a year only and the upkeep is not demanding.

The initiative of the collective of the VPA (Military Political Academy) library encourages us to hope that this first practical and successful effort will not remain isolated, but that it will contribute to the rapid development of compact storage methods in accordance with the best principles of the economic organization of storage areas.

1. See Parts Two and Three. Compare also the experiments which have been made in the following libraries: Trinity College, University of Dublin; Bodleian, Oxford University; and the British Museum, as described by Richard Garnett in "The Sliding-Press in the British Museum," *The Library*, Ser. 1, III (October, 1891), 414-20.

2. The newest reproductions of the storage space arrangement in the British Museum were published by F. N. Pashchenko in (Ф. Н. Пащенко), "О новых путях организации и оборудования книгохранилищ," Библиотеки СССР Сборник, Вып. 12 (1959), 207, 208.

3. From a personal letter received by me in 1958, which also contained a photograph of the equipment.

4. Equipment of this make has been produced in Switzerland since 1947 by Hans Ingold, Ingenieur; in England by J. Glover and Sons, Ltd.; in Sweden by AB Electrolux at Säffle (which since 1953 has produced both a semi-automatic and a fully automatic type; and since 1957 a third type, the so-called Hand-Compactus); and in France by F.A.M.A.C. (Fabrique Alsacienne de Materiel et d'Articles de Classement).

5. The numbers of the Swiss patent as given by R. Stromeyer in *Moderne Probleme des Magazinbaues in Deutschland und seinen Nachbarländern* (Cologne: Greven Verlag, 1958), are: 256988 (which is the basic patent), and 296275, 296940, 282952, 289868, and 297639. The basic patent was granted June 13, 1947. (On page 102 of his book Stromeyer gives the number of the basic patent as 296988, which was evidently a printing error.)

6. See Bibliography for full citations. Stromeyer's description is taken from pages 57-64, *op. cit.*, and the illustrations from pages 140 and 141, *op. cit.*

7. Stromeyer, *op. cit.*, p. 59, says that systems which use two traction cables are not suitable for very deep storage areas because unequal or alternating loading may cause unequal tension which will lead to the overloading of one of the cables. Ostensibly, he states, cables are best because of their maximum possible speed of 11 meters per minute, i.e., 1 meter in 5.4 seconds. This speed is theoretically possible, he continues, because the cable can be grasped by a clamp at any time and any place by simply depressing the lever. He notes that this advantage is, however, partially offset by the clamp slippage at the initial and final pressure on the lever, which may also cause a

noticeably high degree of wear. Under these circumstances, he concludes, the maximum attainable speed of 11 meters per minute cannot be practically utilized.

8. See V. A. Marin's requirements concerning the differentiated dimensions of standardized cases for compact storage of collections in V. A. Marin and A. A. Songina (В. А. Марин и А. А. Сонгина), Определение габаритов стеллажей компактного хранения, Ленинград: 1958.

9. See details in Stromeyer, *op. cit.*, pp. 67-70.

10. Suspension type perpendicular sliding bookcases ("Systeme de rayonnages mobiles B.D.R.") are made by Baudet Donon Roussel. Similar bookcases are also produced by the firm NASH (Nord et Alpes-Schwartz-Haumont). In Germany, compact bookcases are made by Soennecken Bonn and (since 1952) by Otto Kind Grub H—Kotthausen-Cologne. According to Stromeyer, *op. cit.*, note 120, p. 102, Bode-Panzer in Hanover' also plans production of special type compact bookcases.

11. According to the data which I received from J. W. Haden, Librarian of the Bureau International du Travail, Geneva, in a letter dated June 12, 1958, the cases installed after World War II were of the "Ingold" type. 600 meters of these cases cost 30,000 Swiss francs (about 50 Swiss francs per running meter). The storage area load-bearing requirement is 1 [metric] ton per square meter of floor area.

12. Pashchenko, *op. cit.*, pp. 218-24. [See page 128 of this volume.]

13. Described in Åke Kromnow, "Nya typer av kompakta hyllsystem," *Tidskrift för Dokumentation*, XIV, No. 2 (1958), 17-19 [see Kromnow's article beginning on page 141 of this volume], which supplies the additional details that the cases have a free length of 1 meter and depths of 270, 320, 345 or 420 mm.; and that they are designed for files, maps, boxes, etc.

F. N. Pashchenko, on the other hand, states that these manually operated cases are made by the firm "Rosencrens" (evidently E. A. Rosengren). See Pashchenko, *op. cit.*, pp. 222-24 [page 129, this volume]. I saw the Swedish product personally in the Lenin Library in Moscow, but did not note the make. With regard to the construction details it should be mentioned that the rails have a raised area in the center, that there are two rubber covered stops at each end of the floor, and that the contact areas of the bookcase sides are rounded.

14. See F. N. Pashchenko (Ф. Н. Пащенко), Архитектура и строительство библиотечных зданий. Москва: Гос. архит. изд. 1941, 183.

15. For details see my travel report *Studium výstavby sovětských knihoven* [see Bibliography] which also lists original Soviet sources and materials (list of projects, building programs, etc.).

16. See F. N. Pashchenko and G. Meyendorf (Ф. Н. Пащенко и Г. Мейендорф), "Новые пути организации книгохранилищ," Библиотекарь, No. 2 (1956), 26–30, or the discussion by F. N. Pashchenko, *op. cit.*, pp. 227-31 [page 131 of this volume].

17. The equipment installed in the State Historical Library, Moscow. See pp. 83-86, Part Four.

18. D. Gawrecki, *Pro ekonomické využití skladištních prostorů v knihovnách* (Prague: Ustřední Technická Knihovna CSR, 1958).

19. D. Gawrecki, "Novyje puti organizaciji knigochranilišč, *Bibliotekar'*, No. 4 (1959).

Figure 2 is a detail from a drawing which originally appeared in the *First Annual Report of The Midwest Inter-Library Corporation and The Midwest Inter-Library Center* (Chicago, 1950).

The photograph of the MILC storage area (Fig. 3) originally appeared in The Midwest Inter-Library Center's *Second Annual Report* (Chicago, 1951), and was later reprinted in R. Stromeyer, *Moderne Probleme . . . , etc.*

Figure 5 is taken from a brochure issued by Les Forges de Strasbourg, Paris, France, a licensee of Snead & Co. This diagram is reprinted here through the courtesy of Globe Wernicke Co., Cincinnati, Ohio, which purchased Snead & Co. some years ago.

Figures 6, 7, and 19 are taken from R. H. Muller's article "Evaluation of Compact Book Storage Systems," and are reprinted here through the courtesy of the author.

The photographs of the Hamilton Compo Stack equipment (Fig. 8, 9, and 10) originally appeared in the 1956 catalog (AR-26) of The Hamilton Mfg. Co., Two Rivers, Wisconsin, and are reprinted here through the courtesy of that firm.

The illustrations of the Ames Stor-Mor drawers and the Ames Multi-Tier Bookstack (Figs. 11 and 12) were furnished to us by W. R. Ames Co., Milpitas, California. They originally appeared in Ames Catalog BG-57.

Figures 13, 25, 31, 34, 35, 38, 39, 40, 41, 43, 44, 45, 46, and 47 originally appeared in the Soviet journal *Biblioteki SSSR* as illustrations for the Pashchenko article which has been translated as "New Methods for Organizing and Equipping Library Stacks" in this volume. Figure 26 also appeared in the Pashchenko article, and is here reprinted through the courtesy of the Trustees of the British Museum.

The photograph of the Toronto Public Library (Fig. 24) was furnished to us by Mr. Frank Campbell, Chief Librarian.

Figures 28, 29, and 30 were furnished by Ingold Compactus AG, Seefeldstrasse 224, Zurich. Figure 29 first appeared in H. Strahm's article "Eine umwälzende . . . , etc."

Figures 32 and 33 are taken from R. Stromeyer's *Moderne Probleme . . . , etc.*

Figure 36 was taken from the literature of NASH (Nord et Alpes-Schwartz-Haumont, Paris) and was obtained by the author through the courtesy of M. Jean Bleton.

Figure 37 was furnished by M. Paul Rémond of Baudet-Donon-Roussel-RoNeo, Siège Social 27, Bd des Italiens, Paris 2, France.

Figure 42 originally appeared in the Soviet journal *Bibliotekar'*.

All other illustrations are drawings made by the author, Drahoslav Gawrecki.

Bibliography

Aumund, Heinrich. *Hebe-und Förderanlagen; ein Lehrbuch für Studierende und Ingenieure.* 2. Aufl., 2. Band. Berlin: J. Springer, 1926.

> Pages 423-27 of this 1926 publication contain a proposal for the use of a moving conveyor belt system for the storage and distribution of books, archives, etc.

Berghoeffer, Christian. "Bewegliche Repositorien," *Zentralblatt für Bibliothekswesen,* XIII (1896), 152-57.

> Discusses the "sliding press" shelving in the British Museum and the possibilities, in terms of functional and cost considerations, of using this type of equipment in new German library buildings of the time.

Bleton, Jean. "Les magasins à livres dans les bibliothèques francaises du début du 19e siècle à nos jours," *Bulletin des Bibliothèques de France,* I (March, 1956), 183-206.

> Discusses the development of book storage methods in French libraries over the past 150 years, with the author's recommendations for future improvements. Compact shelving, as such, is mentioned only briefly and in the most general terms.

—————. "Les nouvelles bibliothèques municipales de Douai et de Beauvais," *ibid.,* II (May, 1957), 364-88.

> Gives history of the libraries in the cities of Douai and Beauvais and describes their new buildings. Very little on compact shelving.

—————. *Local et mobilier des bibliothèques publiques.* (Institut pedagogique national. Publications. Brochure 605-AL.) Paris: Ministère de l'education nationale. Direction des bibliothèques de France, 1958.

> Chapter 9 contains a short, general discussion of the capacity of bookstacks with both standard and compact shelving, and mentions in brief terms the principal makes of compact shelving in use, or available for use, in France at the time of publication.

Brown, James Duff. *Manual of Library Economy.* 6th ed. by W. C. Berwick Sayers. London: Grafton, 1949.

> Contains some material on compact shelving, mostly in the chapter entitled "Shelving and Accessories."

Ernst, Max. "Die Strafor-Snead-Bausysteme," *Dokumentation, Fachbibliothek, Werksbucherei,* No. 4 (1955-56), pp. 127-31.

> A description of the Snead-Strafor revolving shelf system for archives and libraries, how it is installed, and its advantages and disadvantages from a structural engineering point of view.

Esterquest, Ralph T. "New Directions in Condensed Book Storage," *F.I.D. Review of Documentation*, XVIII (March, 1951), 29-30.

A very brief article by the first Director of The Midwest Inter-Library Center (Center for Research Libraries) about various methods of compact storage, discussed in very general terms.

Gallo, Michelangelo. "Le scaffalature mobili (tipo Acrow, Snead ed Ingold) ed alcune osservazioni sul calcolo dello spazio nei magazzini," *Boletino dell' Instituto di Patologia del Libro*, XV (January-June, 1956), 36-44.

Discusses various methods for computing shelf capacity and the value of using different shelf arrangements in different parts of the library depending on the type of material stored, the amount and kind of usage, etc. Brief descriptions in general terms of some of the principal types of compact shelving.

Garnett, Richard. "The Sliding-Press in the British Museum," *The Library*, Ser. 1, III (October, 1891), 414-20. Reprinted in: Garnett, Richard (ed.). *Essays in Librarianship and Bibliography* (The Library Series, Vol. V). London: G. Allen, 1899.

Historical background of the earliest English systems of compact shelving. Description of the development and installation of the "sliding-press" supplementary shelving in use in the British Museum Library in the late 19th century.

Gawrecki, Drahoslav. "Novyje puti organizacii knigochranilišč," *Bibliotekar'*, (April, 1959), pp. 56-57.

A short discussion of the compact storage proposals made by the Soviet architects Pashchenko and Meyendorf, with some modifications suggested by the author. This material is covered in more detail in the author's work printed in this volume.

——————. *Pro ekonomické využití skladištních prostorů v knihovnách.* Prague: Ustředni Technická Knihovna ČSR, 1958.

Almost all of the material in this pamphlet has been incorporated into the author's work printed in this volume.

——————. *Studium výstavby sovětských knihoven.* Ostrava: Státni vědecká knihovna, 1959.

We do not have a copy of this work, the title of which translates as "Study of the Construction of Soviet Libraries," and is apparently the author's report on his tour of Soviet libraries in 1958.

Gierow, Krister. "Bibliotekens utrymmesproblem; moderna försök till dess losning," *Biblioteksbladet*, XXXVIII, No. 4 (1953), 171-75.

A short, general discussion of the space problems faced by modern libraries and the various attempts which have been made to solve them, including the use of microfilm, microcards, and certain types of compact shelving.

Hill, Francis John. "Compact Storage of Books; a Study of Methods and Equipment," *Journal of Documentation*, XI (December, 1955), 202-16.

This article has been reprinted in this volume (Appendix E).

Howard, J. V. "Aberdeen University. Electrically Operated Shelving," *Liaison; Library Association News-Sheet*, (April, 1958), p. 127.

A very brief (less than one page) description of the new extension of the Aberdeen (Scotland) University Library, which has installed Compactus equipment in an underground book storage area.

Kaiser, Lisa. "Ein neues Regalsystem," *Nachrichten für Wissenschafliche Bibliotheken*, VI (May, 1953), 116-20.

> A short discussion of the main features of the Compactus equipment.

Kromnow, Åke. "Nya typer av kompakta hyllsystem," *Tidskrift för Dokumentation*, XIV, No. 2 (1958), 17-19.

> A translation of this article has been printed in this volume under the title: "New Types of Compact Shelving Systems" (Appendix C).

————————. "Rorliga bokhyllor; nya försök att lösa ett gammalt problem," *ibid.*, IX, No. 6 (1953), 71-75.

> A translation of this article has been printed in this volume under the title: "Movable Bookshelves: New Efforts to Solve an Old Problem" (Appendix B).

Lesyuk, E. and Sabitov, A. (Лесюк, Е. и Сабитов, А.). "Опыт применения передвижных металлических стеллажей," Библиотекарь, No. 8 (1958), 37–38.

> A very short description of the compact sliding shelves in the State Historical Library of the Russian Soviet Federated Socialist Republic.

Marin, V. A. (Марин, В. А.). Компактное хранение библиотечных фондов странах Западной Европы и Америки (Краткая памятная записка). Ленинград: 1957. стройопис (typescript).

————————. О повышении вместимости книгохранилищ. Ленинград: 1957. стройопис (typescript).

> We have been unable to obtain copies of these two unpublished manuscripts. They are very short, and undoubtedly much of the material contained in them is covered by the Marin and Songina article listed below.

Marin, V. A. and Songina, A. A. (Марин, В. А. и Сонгина, А. А.). Определение габаритов стеллажей компактного хранения. Ленинград: 1958. стройопис (typescript).

> In two parts. In the first part, V. A. Marin discusses methods for determining the optimum height of shelves and bookcases, and in the second part, A. A. Songina discusses methods for determining optimum widths.

Muller, Robert Hans. "Compact Storage Equipment; Where to Use it and Where Not," *College and Research Libraries*, XV (July, 1954), 300-307.

> A short, but comprehensive discussion of the principal advantages and disadvantages of compact shelving in general and of the various factors a librarian should think about when considering the installation of compact shelving, which the author sums up as follows: (1) cost of shelving per linear foot; (2) mechanical functioning of the equipment; (3) relative accessibility and visibility of books; (4) efficiency in the shelving, collecting and shifting of books; (5) ease of shelf labeling;

(6) adaptability of the equipment to the floor area under consideration; (7) adjustability of shelves and drawers; (8) hazards and safety features; (9) relative quietness and noisiness in operation; (10) appearance; (11) adaptability to non-book uses; and (12) reconvertibility to noncompact storage if desired or necessary.

——————. "Evaluation of Compact Book Storage Systems," in: *Proceedings of the 1954 ACRL Building Plans Institute* ("ACRL Monograph" No. 11), pp. 77-93. Chicago: Association of College and Research Libraries, 1954.

This article has been reprinted in this volume (Appendix F).

Munthe, Wilhelm. "Kompakte Bokmagasiner," *Nordisk Tidskrift för Bok-och Biblioteksväsen*, X (1923), 24-30.

A description of some compact shelving installations (mostly in Britain) in the early 1920's.

Ottemiller, John Henry. "Yale Divinity Library Creates Shelf Space with Pioneer Plan," *Pioneer* (a publication of Remington Rand's Library Bureau), XVI (November- December, 1953), 6-8.

A very short description of the installation of compact four-way stacks in the Yale Divinity School Library.

Pashchenko, F. N. (Пащенко, Ф. Н.). Архитектура и строительство библиотечных зданий. Москва: Гос. архит. изд. 1941.

We have only that small part of this work (less than one page) which relates to compact shelving. It is very general in nature and the material is covered much more fully in the Pashchenko article printed in this volume (Appendix A).

——————. "О новых путях организации и оборудования книгохранилищ," Библиотеки СССР Сборник, Вып. 12. Москва: Библ. им. Ленина 1959. 199–234.

A translation of this article has been printed in this volume under the title: "New Methods for Organizing and Equipping Library Stacks" (Appendix A).

Pashchenko, F. N. and Meyendorf, G. (Пащенко, Ф. Н. и Мейендорф, Г.), "Новые пути организации книгохранилищ," Библиотекарь, No. 2 (1956), 26–30.

A short, general discussion of compact shelving. Contains proposals for model installations which are discussed fully in the Pashchenko article printed in this volume (Appendix A).

Petrov, I. (Петров, И.). "Устранить недостатки в проектировании и строительстве библиотечных зданий," Библиотекарь, No. 9 (1956), 5–9.

Descriptions of and critical comments on several new Soviet library buildings. Very little on compact shelving.

——————. "Строятся новые здания библиотек," Библиотекарь, No. 6 (1958), 51–54.

A short, general discussion of new library construction in the Soviet Union, with a brief mention of the Pashchenko-Meyendorf designs for compact shelving.

Piasecki, Wladyslaw. "Wrażenia biblioteczne z Moskwy i Leningradu," *Przegląd Biblioteczny*, XXVII (January, 1959), 23-29.

A description of a trip by the author to Leningrad and Moscow, during which he discussed the problems of library construction in general with various Soviet authorities. Very little on the specifics of compact shelving.

Predeek, Albert. "Das moderne englische Bibliothekswesen," Beih. 66, *Zentrablatt für Bibliothekswesen,* Leipsig, 1933.

A short discussion, in general terms, of some compact storage installations in Britain in the early 1930's.

Przybylo, Zofia. "Zwarte magazynowanie zbiorow w bibliotekach," *Przegląd Biblioteczny,* XXVII (January, 1959), 29-44.

A clear, comprehensive discussion of compact shelving in general. Includes a short discussion of the research done by V. A. Marin in the Saltykov-Shchedrin Library in Leningrad and F. N. Pashchenko in the Lenin Library in Moscow and the difference in the methods of these two Soviet authorities.

Rider, Fremont. *Compact Book Storage.* New York: Hadham Press, 1949.

An influential and widely-cited work in the literature of compact storage. In this work, Rider was mostly concerned with the possibilities of achieving more compact storage of library materials on conventional shelving, but he included a short general discussion of certain types of movable compact shelving.

Schmidt, Aloys. "Der Neubau des Staatsarchivs Koblenz," *Archivalische Zeitschrift,* LIII (1957), 85-96.

A detailed history of the Federal Archives in Koblenz, Germany, and a description of its new building completed in 1956. Contains a brief mention of the compact shelving which was installed in one part of the new building.

Sebestyén, Gezá. "A tömor raktározás," *A Könyvtáros* (1957). pp. 515-18.

A good, but brief article on the principal types of compact shelving. Most of the material in this article is covered more fully in the material printed in this volume.

Strahm, Hans. "Eine unwälzende Neuerung in Magazinsystem," *Nachrichten der Vereinigung Schweizerischer Bibliothekare,* XXXI (November-December, 1955), 161-65.

A detailed description of the Compactus installation in the City and University Library of Bern, Switzerland.

Stromeyer, Rainald. *Moderne Probleme des Magazinbaues in Deutschland und seinen Nachbärlandern* (Arbeiten aus dem Bibliothekar-Lehrinstitut des Landes Nordrhein-Westfalen, Heft 15). Cologne: Greven Verlag, 1958.

A very full and detailed discussion of the Compactus-Ingold equipment, including a comparison between that equipment and the Snead (revolving) type. The author concludes that, in general, Compactus shelving is preferable to the Snead type, being more adaptable and more compact. A considerable part of the description of the Compactus equipment also appears in the Gawrecki work printed in this volume.

Tell, Björn. "Rörliga bokhyllor i bibliotek," *Tidskrift för Dokumentation,* X, No. 2 (1954), 20-21.

A translation of this article has been printed in this volume under the title: "Movable Bookshelves in Libraries" (Appendix D).

Willers, Uno. "Utrikesdepartmentets arkiv i sitt nya hus," *Från Departmentet Och Nämder,* XIV (1952), 261-65.

A description of the reorganization of the archives of the Swedish Ministry of Foreign Affairs, with a brief mention of the compact shelving installed in the new building.

Wilson, Louis Round, and Tauber, Maurice F. *The University Library.* 2d. ed. New York: Columbia University Press, 1956.

A standard work on the University library, its organization, function and administration. Contains a short, general discussion of compact shelving in the chapter entitled "Buildings and Equipment."

Yale University, School of Medicine. Yale Medical Library. *Annual Report, 1951-52.*

A discussion of the savings in space to be achieved in the Yale Medical Library by various compact storage methods—narrowing the aisles, shelving by size, etc. Little discussion of specific types of compact shelving.

New Methods for Organizing and Equipping Library Stacks

F. N. Pashchenko

In view of the current growth of book holdings of our libraries, the question of the rational organization of book storage and of the most economical use of space in library stacks is of vital importance.

In the majority of libraries an extreme lack of space is evident, especially for stacks. Because of the lack of room for new arrivals, books are put on shelves which are sometimes crudely prepared, and these shelves are placed in the stacks more or less at random, wherever there happens to be room. This interferes with the correct organization of work and is dangerous in the event of a fire.

Very often it is impossible to enlarge library buildings in proportion to the increase in holdings, since reconstruction of the building or the addition of new building space is more often than not impossible without causing the destruction of the unified architectural composition of the building.

What remains to be done, then, if it is impossible to provide such libraries with more stack space in the near future?

To answer this question we must acquaint ourselves with the manner in which library stacks have been built and equipped in the past, and what is more important, we must discover whether they correspond to modern requirements.

As is well known, in most libraries books are kept on open shelves which are usually arranged in parallel rows with passages from 75 to 80 cm. in width between the rows. The normal height of the shelves (190 to 205 cm.) permits taking books from the uppermost shelf. Single-faced shelves may be placed along the walls. Within the rooms themselves, between the aisles, the shelves are double-faced. Normally the shelves are broken up by upright supports into 1-meter sections (they are normally not made longer than this, since shelves with a 2-cm. thickness would bend under the weight of the books). Single-faced sections have six or seven 1-meter shelves, while double-faced sections have twelve or fourteen 1-meter shelves. Under these conditions, for each section of double-faced shelving, and counting all aisles and approaches, 1.56 square meters of floor space are utilized, of which only about 30 percent is actually used for the shelves themselves.

The question naturally arises as to whether it is permissible to use on the average 70 percent of the floor space of library stacks for aisles between shelves which usually contain a considerable quantity of printed works that are rarely called for, especially considering the present lack of space both in old library buildings and in library buildings now under construction.

It is quite clear that the answer can only be a negative one.

It seems that the degree of usage of different parts of the stacks of a library must become the basis for selecting the most rational arrangement of shelves. For holdings which are in active use by librarians, or that are open to be used freely by readers, we must consider the usual wide spacing of shelves as necessary.

For holdings, however, that are rarely requested, or that are almost never used, a more compact arrangement of shelves must be undertaken—one that would considerably increase the capacity of the area of the stacks in which they are stored.

Now let us examine how, and in which libraries, depending on the way in which their holdings are used, it is possible to streamline the organization of library stacks.

Due to the intense use of the holdings in the majority of the popular libraries, it is expedient in these libraries to use only the standard arrangement of shelves in parallel rows with aisles between. Where the readers do not have free access to the shelves the aisles should be from 75 to 80 cm. in width, but where there is free access, aisles must be 100 to 120 cm. wide. The loss of about 70 percent of the area due to the space taken up by aisles in the first case, and of 80 to 85 percent in the second, is justified by the large turnover of the holdings, and by the fact that librarians or readers are constantly working between the ranges.

This type of organization of book storage is characteristic for central city libraries which have holdings up to 100,000 units.

A different situation may be observed in the stacks of the giant public libraries—district, provincial, and [Soviet] Republic libraries. In district and provincial libraries the holdings at the present time frequently reach 500,000, and in some cases over one million units, and in Republic libraries the holdings may number as many as two million units.

The yearly increase in holdings at the present time in libraries with up to one million units is about 5 percent of the total holdings, and from 3 to 4 percent in the larger libraries. Therefore the planning and building of their stacks must include reserved space in order to guarantee the accommodation of the growth in holdings over a 25 to 40 year period (the usual term of use of a building before reconstruction is necessary).

This large growth of holdings leads to the situation where, when such stacks are equipped with standard stationary shelves, they soon become extremely uncomfortable to work in and very expensive to maintain and operate.

This all tends to indicate that at the present time, as never before, it is absolutely necessary to find a more rational and economical form of storing holdings, especially in the largest of our libraries. However, for the active part of the holdings which are most frequently used by librarians (and, where there are open stacks, by readers as well), the standard arrangement of shelves in parallel rows with aisles between is still necessary.

The distribution of shelves in the so-called magazine stacks which have existed since the middle of the 19th century was considered completely adequate and economical for even the largest libraries of the past, the holdings of which did not exceed 500,000 units. But when the holdings of several giant libraries came to exceed one million units, the disconnectedness of the stacks, and the distance of many of its parts from the place where the books were distributed, became serious hindrances in serving the readers. The use of space for aisles, and also the requirement in those days for natural lighting in the stacks, determined the well-known norm of placing from 300 to 500 books on each square meter of floor space, or 150 units for each cubic meter of building area.

This extreme growth and expansion of the stacks could not help but cause complications in the delivery of books to the place where they were distributed to the reader and, consequently, a lengthening of the time needed to satisfy the reader's needs. At the same time the expansion of the stacks forced many librarians to walk as much as several kilometers during the course of a working day in searching for and delivering books to the point of distribution.

With the aim of eliminating these faults in the serving of readers and in the interest of the more efficient organization of the librarians' work it became necessary to introduce mechanical transportation to speed up and simplify the delivery of books from distant shelves. This, however, gave rise to further expenditures in the construction and use of the building.

Nor was it possible to avoid those organic insufficiencies which are inherent in every "magazine" library with conventional shelving and natural lighting, even in the stacks of the new building of the Lenin State Library of the USSR. The planning of this library began in 1928, when there was as yet no practical experience in the construction of the huge stacks required. During the entire period of planning and construction of this library, which was completed only in 1959, there were no essential changes introduced as far as the more compact arrangement of shelves is concerned. As a result, the main body of the "magazine" stacks of the library is, at the present time, already completely filled, and the critical question has now arisen as to how and where new materials are to be stored. These new materials comprise, in a year, more than 700,000 units of various types of publications (3.3 to 3.6 percent of the entire holdings of the library).

Many of our other large libraries have found themselves in the same position: the Library of the Academy of Sciences of the USSR, the Library of the Academy of Sciences of the Ukrainian SSR, the State Historical Library, and others.

Large foreign libraries are also faced with the problem of overcrowding.

Libraries of capitalistic countries, with few exceptions, are doing little if anything to increase the capacity of their overcrowded stacks. The exceptions are England, Sweden and the United States, where questions of compact storage of books in the stacks are being studied intensively, and where various means of compact shelf arrangement are being contrived. In these countries, many innovations are being tested in actual practice, especially the construction of experimental library buildings. All this is very interesting and can be very instructive for us.

In the Soviet Union the capacity of stacks, up to the present time, was increased only through the construction of auxiliary buildings, or by adding new stories with tiers for additional shelving. But this type of solution destroys the architectural composition of the building, and the new additions, in diminishing the ground area available to the library, usually deprive it of a service area [for trucks, deliveries, etc.] or, what is still worse, partially destroy the landscaping around the building. These defects can be avoided by putting stacks in the so-called light courts—if the building has them. This means of expanding stacks is widely known from the example of the Library of Congress in Washington, D.C., in which all four light courts were built up with multitiered shelves which more than doubled the original capacity of the stacks. This method of enlarging stacks is the most effective in the sense of increasing storage capacity. It is also one of the least expensive, since when it is used there is no necessity for building walls, but only for constructing supports for covering the tiers and for the roof. This method was suggested by the author of this article in 1940 for expanding the stacks of the Library of the Academy of Sciences of the USSR in Leningrad.

This method of expanding stacks should therefore be borne in mind by libraries having buildings with fully enclosed courts, and also buildings with deeply sunk half-courts (alongside the stacks) which open on one side only. These half-courts can also be used for expanding stacks.

But what is to be done for the more radical expansion of the stacks of our large library buildings when they do not have this type of court and when all their reserves of space and shelving have long since been used?

In foreign practice the way out of this dilemma was, until recently, found in the construction of so-called supplementary stacks built either adjacent to the main library, or at some distance from it. The supplementary stacks of the Library of Congress in Washington were built not far from its main building, in the center of the city. Sometimes, however, supplementary stacks had to be built outside of town. Thus, the Bibliothèque Nationale in Paris built its supplementary stacks in Versailles. Both methods increase the area of the stacks of the old magazine system but require new, separately located buildings.

Supplementary stacks can, of course, be built by us as well. But the question arises: Is it sensible to adhere to the old way of storing books? Won't it simply increase still further the time required to serve readers? Does this method correspond to our modern technical abilities?

The answer can only be negative. This method of expanding stacks demands an impractical use of floor space for the aisles between shelves, requires excessive amounts of cubic ˙space in the building, and consequently increases the cost of construction and of the operation of the stacks.

In the opinion of some librarians, it would be possible to avoid overcrowding library buildings with books, magazines and other items by gradually substituting microphotocopies on film and cards for the original holdings. But it must be remembered that microphotocopying of large holdings (even over a considerable period of time) would cost more than the construction of new stacks.

Taking all this into consideration, it seems that the most practical method of solving the problem of acquiring the space for storing the holdings of large stacks would be to put the following measures into practice:

1. The construction of supplementary stacks in the form of independent buildings in the immediate vicinity of the basic library building, or even at a distance from it, not in the form of the usual stacks, but in the form of special storehouses. These latter would be distinguished by optimal sanitary and working conditions (a temperature of 2° to 4° C. is best for book storage, but inadmissible for people doing any extended work); by simplified construction; and by a more compact and economical arrangement of shelves, etc. In comparison with ordinary library buildings, this setup would be considerably cheaper both in its construction and in its operation. In these storehouses we would be able to store the greater part of those holdings which are rarely used by the readers. Working personnel would spend only short periods of time there.

This suggestion is already being put into practice in our current Soviet construction of large library buildings (for example in the Eastern Branch of the Library of the Academy of Sciences of the USSR in Novosibirsk, the building of the Fundamental Library of Moscow University in Moscow, and in others).

2. The establishment of new systems of organizing and equipping stacks, especially for little-used holdings (some parts of the basic holdings, archives and reserve materials, holdings of Book Chambers [bibliographical processing and information centers]), with more compact shelf arrangements.

These new systems can be combined with the construction of supplementary stacks. The problem of acquiring added shelf space has been solved in practice by the following methods.

The first of these methods consists of the further development of the former "magazine" principle of arranging shelves in parallel rows with aisles. The difference is that in each aisle a movable row of double-faced shelving $(1 + 1)$ is joined tightly to a double-faced stationary row; or to a stationary double-faced row is added, on one side, a movable single-faced row of shelves $(1 + \frac{1}{2})$; or a movable single-faced row is added to each side $(\frac{1}{2} + \frac{1}{2})$. All these supplementary shelves conceal the sides of the stationary shelves in front of which they are placed, and in order to gain access to the stationary shelves it is necessary to move the supplementary shelves across the aisles. These supplementary shelves are therefore equipped with rollers and placed on or suspended from tracks.

During the modernization of the old stacks of the British Museum Library just such supplementary shelves on rollers, arranged to face the basic, permanent shelves, were hung on rails from the ceiling of each tier. (See Fig. 26, page 64.)

In the United States several firms which build and prepare new systems of shelving recently have begun to offer various methods for suspending supplementary shelves and attaching them to the stationary ones, by mounting them on hinges (Fig. 53). These hinges make it possible for the librarian to move the supplementary shelves to a 90° position by swinging the un-fastened end outward on rollers, in somewhat the same way as one opens shutters or door panels.

Parallel to this in the Soviet Union a system was developed for moving supplementary shelves by sliding them along the stationary rows. (See Figs. 43 and 44, pages 90 and 91.)

These means of increasing the compactness of book storage in stacks by increasing the capacity of the basic, stationary

Fig. 53   *Stacks of a library in a new building on a college campus*
in the United States [the Midwest Inter-Library Center in Chicago],
equipped with compactly arranged revolving shelves.

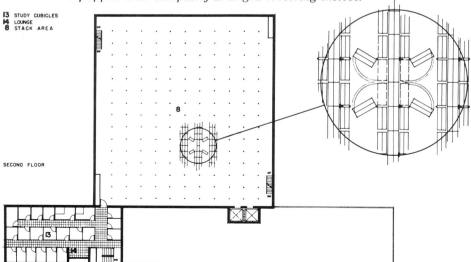

13 STUDY CUBICLES
14 LOUNGE
8 STACK AREA

8

SECOND FLOOR

shelves can be widely used for condensing old, uneconomical, "magazine" stacks, and also for building sensible new stacks.

The second method consists of furnishing new stacks exclusively with rolling shelves, arranged in large, compact groups, out of which any given shelf can be easily moved into an aisle.

This arrangement of rolling shelves in compact groups was used in equipping the library of the International Bureau of Labor (Bureau International du Travail [ILO]) in Geneva, in the Public Library in Toronto, in a number of libraries in Sweden, and in other places.

One of the earliest proposed works of this nature which, unfortunately, was never actually built, was a variant of the plans for reconstructing the library of the British Museum.

The third direction taken in the search for methods of more compact storage is really of no practical importance to us, when compared to the first two methods, since it is based on the use of more complicated and bulky euipment. The outstanding feature of this method consists of the addition of special movable boxes or drawers on alternate shelves of the stationary shelving. Many more books can be stored in these drawers than by the usual method, by placing them in two rows along the length of each pair of alternate shelves. A few libraries took this direction in the construction of special equipment in an attempt to achieve more compact storage many years ago. Despite the wide application of more effective and simpler means of compact storage of library holdings since that time, a number of foreign firms, mainly in the United States, are again making shelves with drawer storage for books.

An increase in the capacity of library stacks by means of drawer storage can, perhaps, be accomplished by the libraries of the Soviet Union during the reconstruction of old magazine stacks. In this case, no great expense would be required for new equipment, since a part of the old, used equipment could be utilized. It is only necessary that the width of the aisles between the shelf ranges be no less than 80 cm., which will allow the librarian to pass around open drawers without difficulty. However, for a more rational use of the work aisles, we recommend that their number be reduced. This would lead to an increase in the number of shelves in a given area, and to a greater compactness of the holdings. In order to do this, all double-faced shelves (both old and supplementary), together with those which have been rebuilt as drawer shelves, must be arranged in pairs (see Fig. 13, page 46).

Let us dwell for a moment on the history of the development of these three methods of condensing stacks.

Supplementary compact stack equipment with hinged or sliding shelves was first used in England. There, in the 19th century, attempts were made to install various systems of movable shelves. The most original of these systems was that suggested by Charles G. Virgo and installed in the Bradford Free Library in England. It was a compact arrangement of hinged shelves in groups of three parallel rows. Virgo's principle has received rather wide application recently in the United States thanks to the technical perfection of this type of system by the firm of Snead & Company, and more especially by Art Metal Inc. Several college and city libraries have been equipped on the same principle (Fig. 53). The essential feature of this system is that from each side of a double-faced section of stationary shelves a set of two movable, hinged shelf cases is hung. These movable cases can be opened like doors, thus allowing access to the cases in the stationary row behind them, and also to the books on the shelves on the inner sides of the movable cases themselves. A roller which moves along a curved metal strip in the floor is fixed to the outer edge of the movable shelves in order to give them additional support when they are opened or closed on their hinges. In comparison with the usual arrangement of double-faced stationary shelves in separate rows, this system increases the capacity of the stacks by 50 to 58 percent. When these hinged shelf elements are used only on one side of the stationary cases, the stack capacity is increased by only 35 percent.

Another form of development of the same method was the system of supplementary shelves used by the British Museum. The shelves were hung from the upper approach aisles, and moved on rollers (see Fig. 26, page 64). In their normal position, the rolling shelves were in front of the stationary cases, so that books were not accessible from the front shelves of these cases until the rolling shelves were moved away. In order to obtain books from the stationary shelves, and from the second row of movable shelves, the rolling shelf was moved by the librarian forward into the aisle (see Fig. 25, page 64). It is difficult to judge the true economic value of this system, since it was used only to enlarge those stacks of the British Museum which were distinguished by their very wide aisles (about 2 meters).

In this same library, in those stacks in which the aisles were considerably narrower, a different means of condensation was

1	2	3	4	5	6	7	8
9	10	11	12	13	14	15	→
16	17	18	19	20	21	22	→
Corridor							
23	24	25	26	27	28	29	→
30	31	32	33	34	35	36	→
37	38	39	40	41	42	43	44

Fig. 54

Diagram of an arrangement of "Stormor" sliding compact shelves.

used, with the aid of those same suspended shelves. These shelves slid sideways, parallel to the ranges, on rollers (and were for this reason called "sliding" shelves) and were placed against the stationary shelves. However these sliding shelves were less spacious, since only one row of shelves was placed in them (they consisted of single-faced, seven-tiered cases). The sliding shelves, just like the roller shelves, existed in the stacks of the British Museum only until 1920, when the stacks were again reconstructed.

This type of system was also used during the reconstruction of other old stacks and the construction of new ones in England and the United States after several improvements which led, mainly, to an increase in the number of sliding rows attached to each stationary row. This type of compact shelf arrangement is known by the name of "Stormor." The firm of J. Glover & Sons, Ltd. in London installed this new system of shelving in the Royal Library in Stockholm. From three to five rows of movable sliding shelves on each side were placed along the stationary rows (Fig. 54). In comparison with the usual spacing of double-faced rows of stationary shelves, this system increases the capacity of stacks having the same area from 63 to 65 percent.

The second method, first used in England, is also related to the older form of compact stack structure. Even before World War I, the stacks of the Bodleian Library in Oxford were successfully reconstructed, and then, somewhat later, the stacks of the Cambridge University Library. In these libraries the firm of W. Lucy and Co. suggested the building of sliding shelves which would raise the previous capacity of each stack by 22 to 23 percent. This compact arrangement of book holdings, although it received favorable recognition at the time, is now considered too expensive, since the system of sliding shelves ("pull-out shelves") required a great number of precision-made elements (casters, guide mechanisms, etc.). Nevertheless, the reconstruction of the stacks of the Oxford and Cambridge libraries had great significance, since it provided the impetus for the further development of the idea of moving separate elements out from the general mass of compactly arranged shelves. This principle has now established itself as a basic one and is in universal use.

In developing this system of compact stacks, the firm of T. E. Foulkes, in England, about 1930 or 1931, suggested double-faced shelves for the Library of the British Museum, arranged in pairs in groups of 14 to 16 units, which were to be rolled out into one of the longitudinal corridors or aisles. The librarians would do this work by hand. Moving freely over the floor on casters, the required 1-meter section of shelving was to be pulled out of the large group with its narrow end forward. This system of movable shelves, requiring an uneconomical width of aisle (each section was 103 to 106 cm. long), was employed in the Mitchell Library in Glasgow, and also in the stacks of the new Toronto Public Library (see Fig. 24, page 62). This compact spacing of shelves, in comparison to the usual spacing of rows of double-faced stationary shelves, increased the capacity of the stacks of the Toronto Public Library by 33 percent.

This system resulted in relatively small savings because of the necessarily wide aisles. The English "Stormor" system improved it considerably, due to the fact that in moving a section of shelves from the group they were moved with the long side forward, rather than the short one. The capacity of stacks equipped with these separately moving, 1-meter sections of shelves, arranged in pairs, is increased by 40 percent in comparison with those stacks with the usual stationary arrangement of shelves. This system is somewhat reminiscent of the nature and direction of the movable supplementary shelves constructed during the first condensation of the old stacks of the Library of the British Museum (see Fig. 25, page 64), although, in that case, the shelves were suspended from movable, rolling frames.

Around 1936 the "Stormor" equipment offered a still more improved system, uniting the 1-meter sections of movable shelves into rows of two, three, and even four sections. This permitted an increase in the number of sections of shelving on any given floor space by almost 100 percent, and correspondingly increased the capacity of the stacks by 93 to 95 percent. It is quite clear that increasing the number of shelf sections on the same floor area (for example, from 24 sections of conventional stationary shelves to 48 compact, movable, rolling sections, joined four to a row) [see Figs. 45 and 47, pages 92 and 94], was possible only by using the aisle space. In an arbitrarily defined area (7.50 by 5, or 37.50 square meters) the obviously surplus area of the aisles occupies 26.68 square meters or almost 70 percent in the conventional system, and in the compact system, only 14.60 square meters, about 36 percent.

However, due to the necessity of frequently moving these blocks of compactly arranged shelves, physical difficulties immediately arose, especially during the first movement, when it was necessary to move out three, or worse, sometimes four paired sections, loaded from top to bottom with books (about 2,000 kg. including the weight of the shelves). Therefore the idea arose of using mechanical force to replace the physical labor of the librarians in moving shelves. After World War II, under the patent of the Swiss engineer Hans Ingold, the rolling shelves began to be propelled by electric motors. Each block of shelves was supplied with an electric motor of ½ to ¾ hp. This permitted moving whole sections of shelves at a time, consisting of a large number of ranges, in order to form an aisle in the required place. Moving these blocks to the required distance, stopping them in time to guarantee the safety of those people who may be in the passage between the shelves, and making electrical connections between them is done automatically or semi-automatically. This system was a great advance in the development of the principles and techniques of constructing compact stacks, and was worked out mainly by the Swedish firm Compactus [author probably refers to AB Electrolux].

Regardless of the fact that rolling, movable shelves were not used in Sweden until 1945-46, this country, at the present time, has moved into first place both in the technical virtues of its equipment for compact storage and in the development of the use of this equipment in libraries, archives, and industrial warehouses. The first institution in Sweden in which a system of rolling movable shelves was installed was the Archive of the Ministry of Foreign Affairs, and the initiator was its director, Dr. Uno Willers. Initially, the English firm of W. Lucy & Co. was called in for the construction of the archive stacks in the reconstructed old building and also in the basement of the new structure. The majority of the stacks which were subsequently set up, however, were equipped by Swedish firms, including the Compactus firm.

The stacks of the library of the International Bureau of Labor in Geneva were also equipped by the [Swiss] Compactus firm. This firm initially envisaged the joining of two sections of double-faced, 14-shelf sections on a common frame equipped with rollers. The use of these units in the library of the International Bureau of Labor guaranteed an increase in the compactness of book placement in a given area of 50 percent (see Fig. 31, page 69, lower row) in comparison with the usual stationary shelf arrangements (see Fig. 31, page 69, upper row). The librarian moves each block or range with the aid of a slight pressure on a lever which engages an electric motor for a set interval of time. When the shelves are moved together, their faces are tightly sealed by rubber tubing which lines their sides, and thus each section forms a sealed unit which isolates the books from the surrounding atmosphere.

The most recent system of equipping compact stacks, again by the Compactus firm, has the cases arranged, not on individual frames, but on a common movable frame which joins from four to six sections of double-faced shelves (see Fig. 34, page 74). The four-section arrangement is the most widely used. Such stacks, in comparison with the stationary arrangement, ensure up to 95 percent condensation of the stored material, since for groups of 10 to 15 ranges (40 to 60 shelf sections), only one aisle between parallel ranges of shelves is necessary. In order to form the aisle in the required place, it is not necessary to move each range separately; the entire group of ranges is moved by a push on the lever. This similtaneous movement of a group of ranges is the reason that all such compact stacks are called "train systems."

The Compactus firm, in setting up the "train system" in buildings especially designed for it, first places all the roller frames on metal strips set into the floor (see Fig. 34, page 74). This ensures the accuracy of their movements up to each other, since on this depends the tight fit of the rows of shelves. After the most exact checks for vertical and horizontal juncture positions, the shelf cases are mounted on the carefully adjusted frames (see Fig. 35, page 75). An electric motor is attached to each block of ranges. A driving system transfers power from the motor to the bookcases. In Fig. 30, page 68 is shown a general view of such compact stacks in use. Such a concentration of shelves gives the greatest possible compactness. The main aisle, running alongside the groups of shelves in the middle of the room, is made very wide (1.40 meters), and is illuminated by natural light.

In order to simplify the use and at the same time lower the expense of roller shelves for the train system, the Swedish firm Rosencrens [author probably refers to E. A. Rosengren AB] in

Gothenburg designed a construction involving the manual moving of the roller shelf sections. This construction recommends itself both as to price and as to the ease and comfort of working with it. For example, it is used in the newly equipped supplementary building of the stacks of the Royal Library in Stockholm, in many other libraries and archives in Sweden, as well as in other countries. The main reason for this success is the precise construction of all the elements and moving parts of the shelf units, which are also distinguished by their exceptionally easy motion. Such library stack equipment obviously will be widely used in our libraries and archives, thanks also to its relatively simple nature.

In recent times a number of American and English firms have been preparing compact shelf equipment in which shelves are replaced by drawers. There is a special sliding apparatus on these shelves which allows for the easy opening of the drawers to their full extent without the danger of removing them completely from the frame. Books are either placed vertically in the drawers or, if they are very large, horizontally. This, however, somewhat complicates the process of finding the books.

In working for the improvement of shelves with movable drawers, American firms are achieving an increase in the capacity of the drawers by gradually freeing them of their side walls, and thus making them more similar to standard shelves. For example, the firm of Hamilton Manufacturing Co. produces movable shelves 18 inches wide. As many books may be stored in each of these drawers as on a conventional shelf 72 inches long (see Fig. 9, page 41). W. R. Ames Co., continuing to work on the improvement of its earlier movable drawer system, has actually reached the point where the shelves have lost the shape of drawers (see Fig. 11, page 43), and they can replace conventional shelves on conventional stationary steel frames.

In the Soviet Union compact book storage was first planned in 1939 by the author of this article, and was intended for the new building of the Library of the Academy of Sciences of the USSR in Moscow (see Fig. 38, page 81). We again suggested this same principle of the arrangement of movable shelves in groups of 24 double-faced sections in the project of the building of the Public Library of the Karelian ASSR in Petrozavodsk (see Figs. 39 and 40, page 82). This project was developed in 1948 by the architect K. Gutin in consultation with the author.

In both projects of compact book storage, the first step was the system of double rows of movable shelves (more exactly

1-meter, double-faced sections) first used in the stacks of the new public library in Toronto. In contrast to the open rolling frames, however, we suggested solid supporting sides for the shelves (like the type shown in Fig. 41, page 83), which completely isolate each separate group of shelves. This ensures the possibility of individual air-conditioning, and also the centralization of dust control and disinfection (for the prevention of mold, etc.).

At the present time the author, in collaboration with the architect G. V. Meyendorf, is continuing to work out plans for the condensing of library stacks in the reconstruction of old libraries and in the building of new library buildings in the Soviet Union. Several new systems of compact shelf arrangement have been developed. Special attention has been devoted to the reconstruction of the uneconomical magazine arrangement which was used for many existing library stacks.

In our first system the aisle width is assumed to be not less than 95 cm. Supplementary single-faced movable sections of "sliding" shelves are placed on one side of each existing, stationary row of shelves (see Fig. 43, page 90). The number of the movable sections equals the number of double-faced sections of each row of the old stationary shelves minus one. It is necessary to omit one movable section in order to form a gap into which the remaining movable sections of the same row may be moved. In this system all the old stationary shelves are retained, and they are used without being rebuilt. Moving the "sliding" sections along the aisle in order to gain access to the books on the stationary shelves will give the librarians little difficulty, even though the operation must be done by hand. The capacity of the stacks after this reconstruction, compared with the conventional magazine stacks with the usual shelf arrangement, is increased for the same floor area by 26 to 28 percent, while funds must be spent only for preparing the supplementary roller shelves.

Very much like the above system is another one, in which single-faced shelves on movable frames are set up on *both* sides of each stationary row (see Fig. 44, page 91). However, in this case the existing shelves must be moved so that after the two rows of single-faced supplementary shelves have been added, the aisles will be no less than 75 cm. wide. In comparison with the usual magazine arrangement, the capacity of the stacks after this type of reconstruction is increased, for the same amount of floor area, by 29 to 33 percent.

It is intended to use this type of construction in the old, uneconomical, so-called iron stacks of the Lenin State Library of the USSR, which was built at the end of the 19th century. Due to the existing width of the aisles (about 115 cm.), the capacity of these stacks will be increased by 80 to 83 percent.

A more radical method of condensing stacks was suggested by us on the basis of using some "pull-out" movable shelves which are joined hermetically to each other on their long sides (see Fig. 40, page 82). This increases the general capacity of the stacks by almost one and one-half times.

In such a system the group of shelves appear as though they are contained within continuous metal boxes which isolate them from the general area of the stacks.

It should be noted that it is possible to achieve still more capacity for stacks by placing the shelves, not with their short sides facing the aisles (which must be in this case from 1.10 to 1.40 meters wide), but with their long sides facing the aisles. This would radically alter the means of grouping shelves, and would allow for moving rows perpendicularly. For this movement a simple pneumatic, or in some cases electric, mechanism can be used. This mechanism must allow several rows to be moved at once. In this system of grouping shelves, it is sufficient to have aisles only 70 cm. wide (see Fig. 46, page 93).

A life-sized experimental model of one double-faced shelf section has been prepared under the supervision of G. V. Meyendorf. It is moved with its narrow end facing outward (see Fig. 41, page 83), and in practice it has completely justified and proved the feasibility and convenience of such a system.

In 1955 G. V. Meyendorf and the author of this article suggested that this system be used for the expansion of the capacity of the old and exceedingly cramped stacks of the State Historical Library in Moscow. All the succeeding work on the reconstruction of these stacks was done according to the general plan of G. V. Meyendorf who was, at the same time, consultant to a number of specialists who were summoned to solve special problems involved in this reconstruction.

In the train shelf system of this project, the shelves are joined in groups of 12 rows. In each of the rows it is possible to form an aisle wherever desired. An interesting innovation here is the mechanism which allows the librarian to move a group of rows of shelves, loaded with books. The "motor" consists of a hand-operated wheel about 40 cm. in diameter on the outside wall of each row. A transmission system, made up of a chain and two gears of different diameters is connected to the rollers of an entire row through their common axle.

The old stacks, currently located in exceedingly high rooms, can accommodate four tiers. In each room, compact equipment has been installed, and this has increased the capacity of the library stacks threefold.

Along with the positive aspects of the construction and use of new compact stacks in the State Historical Library we cannot, however, overlook their deficiencies, such as inaccurate finishing, the lack of insulation of each group of shelves when they are shut off from the remaining space of the stacks, the unsolved problems of lighting the open aisles between shelves, and the mechanical problems of moving the shelf units.

The conversion to the use of compact shelves, placed in large groups in a fully intergrated system, can give the following advantages over the standard magazine arrangement:

Nearly double the old capacity, because the old arrangement of shelves requires, for each section, 1.56 square meters, while the new one needs only from 0.77 to 0.89 square meters.

A decrease by almost half in the cubic area of new stacks, compared with magazine stacks, and, consequently, a reduction in construction expense of about 40 percent.

A considerable lowering of the cost of using the stacks (in electric lighting, ventilation, janitor services, etc.).

An improvement in the storage of the collections due to their storage away from natural light and from dust.

A shortening of the distance from the place of storage to the distribution point for books, and a consequent shortening of the distance which must be traveled by stack workers.

The possibility of more effective sanitary protection within the area of each separate, isolated group of shelves.

The closing off, when required, of each hermetically sealed group of shelves and the local isolation of stored material.

The protection of collections from damage during periods of repair in the stacks, as well as other work which is done by outside personnel (sweeping, repair, fire protection, etc.).

Improved conditions of fire safety for the collections.

Normal natural lighting in all parts of the main aisles of the stacks.

The possibility of allowing readers less dangerous and better controlled access to parts of the stacks.

The possibility of condensing the old stacks currently in use by reducing the superfluous or unused aisle space between the stationary shelves (which may, however, require a corresponding strengthening of the flooring).

In this article we have raised a very important question, one which can no longer be put aside, namely, the question of the method of constructing modern library stacks to meet modern conditions and modern needs.

Movable Bookshelves: New Efforts to Solve an Old Problem

Åke Kromnow
(Translated by Rudolph C. Ellsworth)

Little needs to be written about the lack of space in archives and libraries. We are all well aware of this problem, all too frequently in a very urgent way. Moreover, the problem is common for everyone concerned with storing books, newspapers, documents, and forms of various kinds. In America it has been estimated that the larger libraries double their holdings every 16 years, and in Sweden that the government archives alone now amount to nearly 400,000 running meters of shelving, which roughly corresponds to the distance between Stockholm and Alingsås. The annual growth of the archives of only the central agencies in Stockholm has increased approximately tenfold in 50 years, and the flood of paper and print does not appear likely to decrease. Industrial concerns often have the same problem. Weeding and filming have become quite common measures, but in most cases are only a partial solution to the problem of space. Not all kinds of material can or should be weeded, and the filming of archives is as a rule more expensive than new archive construction. It is not to be wondered then that the question of the more effective use of available premises has become more and more urgent.

In an excellent article in *Norsk Årbok for Bibliotek og Forskning*, Vol. II (1953), 86-92, "Fra boksalen til motorreolen," the recently retired director of the Oslo University Library, Dr. Wilhelm Munthe, described the development of library storage from the armarium—the medieval bookcase with its few parchment manuscripts—to the early reading rooms with tall bookshelves where a stepladder was a necessary implement, then to the later stacks of cast iron with grills instead of floors, and finally to the contemporary "Compactus" system with movable ranges. These contemporary movable bookshelves are the subject of the present discussion.

Bookcases mounted on ball-bearing wheels are nothing new. In his article ["Kompakte Bokmagasiner"—See Gawrecki Bibliography], Wilhelm Munthe reported on the ball-bearing installations that one of the leading library equipment firms in Great Britain, W. Lucy & Co., made at the Cambridge University Library in 1903 and in the underground extension of the Bodleian Library at Oxford in 1912. The system consisted of placing double-faced bookcases close together like books on a shelf. As the double-faced sections ran on wheels in rails either at the top or at the bottom, they could be drawn out the same way a book is taken out of a shelf.

Although the aisle had to be wide enough so that the double section could be drawn out to its full length, the system increased the shelving area in the underground stack of the Bodleian Library to about 66 percent of the floor space. Older shelving systems had not exceeded 45 percent. However this "draw out" system was not widely accepted in spite of the saving in space and with its expansion of 1946 the Bodleian Library returned to standard stack sections. But then, to cite Munthe, "the Rockefeller Foundation paid the bill."

Shelves of the type just described were already being discussed around 1900.[1] The "swing" system (hinged shelving) was also known at an early stage. This system consists of sections of shelves which can be opened like doors thus giving access to fixed sections behind. A modern version of this type was installed at the Midwest Inter-Library Center [now the Center for Research Libraries] in Chicago. Double-faced sections were hung on each side of stationary sections in units made up of three layers. The middle, double-faced, standard section is fixed and both outer sections swing out like doors. This system allows a saving of 66 percent of the floor space compared to the regular type of shelving. The system is called Snead Compact Storage and is still in use in the United States.

In 1936 T. E. Foulkes in England hit upon the idea of placing the shelf sections end to end and then have them slide sideways instead of standing them closely packed lengthwise as in the Bodleian Library. A standard range of fixed sections is placed innermost at the greatest distance from the corridor. In front of

1. Fremont Rider, *Compact Book Storage* (New York: Hadham Press, 1949), pp. 30 ff.

this range are set one or more rows of cases consisting of movable units about 1 meter wide. To reach the inner units, the intervening sections need only be moved to one side.

Patents are pending for the Foulkes Mobile Storage System and it is manufactured at the present time by a firm in London. It is usually sold under the name Stormor. Munthe calls it the "sliding" system. It has been used in Belgium and Holland as well as in England. Firms such as Lloyds Bank and the Northern Assurance Company in London, whose space is very limited, have found in the Stormor system a means to economize on expensive storage space. Even in very small areas where only a couple of narrow sections of rolling shelves can be installed, the space can be more fully used, with shelving capacity increased by 100 percent or more. In 1951 representatives from the Swedish Ministry for Foreign Affairs studied the Stormor installations in these two firms for the purpose of possibly installing the system in the new archives of the Foreign Ministry behind the Crown Prince's Palace [now the building of the Ministry for Foreign Affairs] at Gustav Adolf's Square in Stockholm. After the National Board of Building and Planning found that the additional costs for the English shelving units would be amortized in about 10 years through savings gained by not having to rent additional storage space, the greater part of the Foreign Ministry's archive was equipped with Stormor cases. In spite of a rather ample fitting out of the premises to begin with, it was found that the archive space could be increased 50 percent with the Stormor installation, thus the ministry's other storage areas in the city could be given up and the entire archive for the Ministry could be kept under one roof. This is believed to have been the first time that moving shelves on ball-bearing wheels were installed in Sweden. The agency firm P. Larm is one of the dealers for the Stormor system in Sweden.

As noted above, Stormor units are mounted on ball-bearing wheels. If higher tiers are desired, the sections can also be run on overhead rails, and this prevents the units from becoming top-heavy. There is no risk of persons being crushed between the sections. It is obvious of course that the more compact the installation is made, the greater the number of sections that must be pushed aside to reach the innermost cases. Thus in installing Stormor units, consideration must be given to ease of access versus demand for shelf space. In the archive of the Swedish Foreign Ministry there are installations containing from 6 to 60 movable cases. The smaller installations are reserved for material that is frequently used; the larger are of course kept for material that is less frequently used.

The movable shelving units considered up to this point have all been hand-operated. After World War II, a Swiss engineer, Hans Ingold, patented a system of shelving units that can be moved by electric power. These are double-faced ranges packed close together with the short ends at right angles to the wall. Space for only one aisle parallel to the row of sections of bookcases is needed. An electric gear motor of one or two horsepower is also needed.

The movement of the motor is transferred by a moving rack located under the movable ranges. At the open end of each row (which are more or less standard range lengths) is a lever to couple the range to the driving rod. For example, if the lever on range number 10 is lowered, a steel pin drops into the rack and ranges 1-10 move to the right while ranges 11-15 stand still. Thus an aisle is formed between rows 10 and 11. Rubber baffles on the ranges allow close packing and seal out light and dust when the system is not being used by the staff. Safety features are provided to eliminate the risk of one person operating the system while another is in between two ranges. When the lever of one range is down, a circuit breaker must be set at the control panel before the motor will start. After the aisle between the ranges is opened, which takes 5 to 10 seconds, the electrical system is interlocked so that no person can start the motor as long as anyone is in the aisle. As soon as the work in the open aisle is done, the interlock is turned off by a special circuit breaker in the open aisle. Such a device is mounted on every range. Thus the person who closes the aisle must first check to see that nobody is in the aisle. The motor is then started by a main switch on the control panel. If this does not function right away, the system is again interlocked by a time clock set for the interval it takes (about 5 seconds) to get from the interlock switch at the range to the circuit breaker at the control panel. This procedure ensures that no unauthorized person can come into the aisle while the ranges are moving together. When the installation is closed the range is uncoupled from the driving rack and a new aisle may be opened.

The detailed procedure employed every time the system is used, and the fact that it can be used only by one person at a time, mean that the completely automatic "Compactus" system, by the manufacturer's own statements, is most suitable for material that is not frequently used. In addition to installations in Switzerland, it is used in Germany, Belgium, and Holland. To cope with the inconveniences just mentioned Ingold has recently given the system a new design, the semi-automatic "Compactus," which is suitable for material in frequent use. In this newer installation a small electric motor (½ to ¾ hp.) drives an endless steel cable to which the ranges can be coupled for movement to both sides. This is done by moving the lever on the end of the range in one direction or the other. As long as the lever is down the ranges are in motion. The system can thus be used continuously without going to the control panel every time the ranges are to be moved, and the low power of the motor ensures that no one will be crushed between the rows of cases. A disadvantage is that the number of ranges must be limited so that the weight of the rolling "train" of bookcases will not become dangerous for the person who stands in the way. Thus the semi-automatic installations are not built for useful loads of greater than 20 metric tons [approximately 22 short tons], or in double installations (the motor is the same for both) for 40 metric tons [approximately 44 short tons]. Both types of the "Compactus" system are now made in Sweden by AB Electrolux.

Many shelving systems have been tried during the past hundred years, but as far as can now be seen in this area the new shelving units mounted on ball-bearing wheels have probably brought about something of a revolution in both industrial and academic installations. Since the Ministry for Foreign Affairs has installed its moving shelves, Stormor and "Compactus" systems have been installed or ordered at several places in Sweden. Which system is best is a question of usage and costs that must be decided for each installation. The answer requires careful weighing of several factors. It may often happen that a combination of various systems proves to be the most effective.

New Types of
Compact Shelving Systems

Åke Kromnow
(Translated by Rudolph C. Ellsworth)

In 1953 a report appeared in this journal on various systems of movable, compact shelving systems including the "sliding" (Stormor) and the "train" systems ("Compactus") [see article on page 135]. Both of these systems were new in the Nordic countries at the time. This article was supplemented by a report by Björn Tell on management and air conditioning of movable shelves [see article on page 145].

Since the publication of these articles compact shelving systems have advanced considerably even here in Sweden. However the traditional shelving has by no means outlived its usefulness. The choice of appropriate shelving systems has become a question of weighing a number of economic and practical factors where individual circumstances in each particular situation are decisive. One solution which would be suitable for all archives and libraries cannot be attained.

The two compact systems now competing in Sweden are the "E. A. Rosengren" system and the "Compactus-Ingold" system.

The Rosengren system is based on the first compact shelving to be used in the Nordic countries, the English Stormor system installed in the archive of the Ministry for Foreign Affairs in 1952. After the patent on this system expired, E. A. Rosengren AB in Gothenburg has made movable units according to the "sliding" system as well as the "train" system and the "draw-out" system. The principles for these different types of shelving were given in my [1953] article.

Common to the Rosengren moving shelves is that each unit or section of shelves is mounted on ball-bearing wheels which run on rails in the floor. Thus this shelving is easy to move by hand. Soon uprights are to be produced in which the holes for fastening the shelves will not be visible from the ends of the cases.

The other kind of compact shelving available in the Scandinavian countries is the original Swiss "Compactus, system Ingold." As noted in the [1953] article, AB Electrolux introduced to Sweden two types of "Compactus" shelving, the automatic and the semi-automatic. The latter of these has become the more popular here because it (1) suffices for installations which need not be too extensive, (2) requires a smaller motor, and (3) is easier to operate than the completely automatic type. An excellent opportunity to study both types of "Compactus" is now available at the Royal Military Record Office where a projected 11-story tower with standard stack installations was reduced to a four-story building by means of the use of "Compactus" units.

A characteristic of "Compactus" is that the bookcases are moved by electric power with or without the help of manpower. The motion of the motor is transferred by a moving rack placed under the movable units. By a lever at the open end side of each row of one or more sections, this range can be coupled to the rack and thus moved sideways.

Recently, however, the AB Electrolux factory at Säffle has put on the market a third type of the Ingold "train" system, called "Hand-Compactus." This is intended for smaller installations in offices and differs from the other "Compactus" units principally in that, like the Rosengren units, it is not motor driven but is hand-operated. The movable section is placed on a platform or frame which is laid on the floor and which has built-in rails. The cases glide easily on these. An advantage is that this system can be locked.

The shelf units have a free width of 1 meter and the depth may be specified at 270, 320, 345, or 420 mm. The system is designed for binders and file boxes as well as various sizes of file holders.

An advantage of the compact "train" systems is that the archive material is better protected from light and dust, and also that when the system is opened the units serve as traditional bookshelves. It seems to be characteristic of the "Compactus" and Rosengren "train" systems that loosely packed documents and books run less risk of falling out when the cases are moved. [This is undoubtedly due to the fact that the movement is perpendicular to the long side of the case and there are therefore no lateral movements which would tend to tip the books on their sides.]

Thus when storage space is limited, the compact shelving systems can offer an effective and aesthetically satisfactory solution to the space problem often so urgent in archives and libraries. The advantage of decreasing the time and difficulty of access by concentrating the location of the material should also be considered. On the other hand where space is available and frequency of use is great, the traditional shelving which is easy to reach and well-arranged is still as a rule the best solution.

Movable Bookshelves in Libraries

Björn Tell
(Translated by Rudolph C. Ellsworth)

Under the title "Movable Bookshelves: New Efforts to Solve an Old Problem" [see p. 135], Åke Kromnow discussed various types of movable shelves and pointed out in conclusion that the new shelves mounted on ball-bearings ought to "bring about something of a revolution within both industrial and academic installations." Whoever has had occasion in recent years to follow developments in the reorganization of storage facilities has good reason to be gratified by the attempts to apply modern methods from industry and trade within the academic world.

For the sake of completeness, however, it should perhaps be pointed out that the system of movable cases is not merely a matter of handling library space; at the same time consideration must be given to the problem of servicing the material stored. The installation of one or more mechanical and space-saving methods (movable shelving, for example) is only what is called by C. G. Weman in his book *Moderna lager i industri och grosshandel* (Modern Storage in Industry and Wholesale Trade) (Stockholm, 1953) a "point solution" for storage problems, and it becomes effective and economical only when it can also be applied smoothly to rational methods of service and the movement of books. From the warehousing point of view a large bookstack is a rather scattered and inefficient storage area and thus makes greater demands on supervision and the distribution of work. However, in a depository library such as the Midwest Inter-Library Center [now called the Center for Research Libraries] in Chicago, the storage problem is dominant. For that library, therefore, where the question of economizing on space is dominant, this has been found to be best achieved by a system of movable shelving. The volume of circulation is not large and the delivery of books desired can be satisfied within a reasonable time by a small work force.

On the other hand, in a large research library with a large circulation the service and transport aspects become quite important. Delivering and shelving books in a modern library several stories high, with storage, administration, and service functions divided up on the various floors, can be made effective only by a carefully thought-out system of bringing the books together and moving them about. In the new library at the Bodleian this work has been mechanized by a combination of pneumatic tubes, conveyor belts, endless chain elevators, and book trucks. Within the framework of this service mechanism, which functions as quickly and carefully as a watch, no system of movable shelving yet developed can be accommodated.

Referring to an article by Wilhelm Munthe, the former director of the Royal University Library in Oslo, Kromnow begins his account with Munthe's description of the rolling cases at the Bodleian Library and he concludes this description with the words: "However, this draw-out system was not widely accepted in spite of the saving in space, and with its expansion in 1946 the Bodleian Library returned to standard stack sections. But then, to cite Munthe, 'the Rockefeller Foundation also paid the bill.'" Such financing allowed a certain generosity; even so, the purely economic aspect of book delivery necessitated a return to regular shelving. It may be observed, moreover, that the British Museum, which has had the "sliding" system in some stacks, now is abandoning it. Thus a saving of space is not the most important factor for determining whether movable shelves should be used in research libraries.

There may be good reason, however, for considering certain problems of a more special kind. These problems are connected with the fact that the product stored is books, which vary in size as well as in "sensitivity," and are not to be compared with either finished or semi-finished industrial products or standardized archive folders. Movable shelving systems for the storage of books demand complicated arrangements and great care in handling. Even slight jolts and movements of the sections may cause the books to slide or be displaced on the shelves, which means that they can easily be crushed or ripped apart. Both the Bodleian and British Museum libraries have had experiences of this kind.

In planning the use of movable shelves for books it is difficult at long range to determine the limit for overloading. In addition, mechanical installations have the shortcoming that their useful life is considerably shorter than the library building itself. In general, a library is built for the purpose of long-range storage and no special replacement fund, similar to those provided for movable inventories in industry, is available. To get equipment replacements after 20 years or so is often very difficult. This aspect of the problem may be illustrated by the situation at the British Museum. The cases there ran on rails in the ceilings, which despite their thickness, sometimes buckled under the load. That means were finally obtained to replace them is probably due to the bomb which hit that part of the building during the blitz of World War II.

Dampness is one of the worst enemies of books. Paper and leather, as well as adhesives of various kinds, are affected by dampness. A certain amount of circulation of air always takes place in a regular bookstack, and great changes in the relative humidity scarcely affect the book stock if normal circumstances prevail. However, in a stack of compact shelving an increase of the relative humidity in the air during a certain period can cause serious damage to paper and binding by forming mold. During war or a period of blockade it may become difficult to control the humidity content. The Bodleian offers an example of this. There the underground book store is under the north lawn as seen from the Radcliffe Camera and is in two levels with space estimated for more than a million volumes. The even temperature distribution throughout the year in this underground book store should normally be advantageous. However, during World War II the heating was reduced and with this the relative humidity increased so that moisture condensed on the walls of the structure. The result was a serious formation of mold. Efforts were made later to check this by the use of heat and air conditioning. However, it has proved difficult to arrange effective ventilation in such a compact stack. Replacement with regular shelving has proved beneficial.

A compact shelving system therefore requires more careful air conditioning than regular shelving. Newly bound books are particularly sensitive to unfavorable changes in the relative humidity. Damage caused by moisture as well as the effect of drying are thus more difficult to find and control in compact systems of movable cases. In conclusion, it should be emphasized that movable shelving must be viewed in the context of storage as well as that of handling. What is gained in space may be lost in accessibility or by injury to the material stored.

The Compact Storage of Books: A Study of Methods and Equipment

F. J. Hill

Lack of shelf room is no new problem to the librarian. In the past, relief for overcrowded shelves has traditionally been sought in the extension of existing buildings, or the construction of new ones. Where neither method could be adopted to provide for the normal growth of stocks or where accessions were unexpectedly and greatly augmented, for example, by the receipt of a large collection of books, severe difficulties often resulted, and the annals of libraries refer often enough to material lying unshelved or housed in totally unsatisfactory quarters. Once the shelf had evolved from the book-rests of the medieval library nearly four centuries were to pass before any further significant step was taken in storage methods.

With the growth of library stocks the height of shelving came to be increased, access to the upper levels being afforded by galleries, and during the nineteenth century cast-iron construction was introduced, to be superseded in its turn by steel and concrete. Much space continued to be unprofitably taken up by the gangways and aisles required to give access to shelving, and it was eventually realized that the proportion of shelving in relation to the total volume of a book store could be increased by using movable presses in addition to fixed ones. Various suggestions were put forward which depended on the use of some form of shelving capable of being easily moved aside to provide access to part of the books it contained, or to those in fixed shelving which it supplemented. One variety, proposed by Mr. Gladstone, was to consist of wheeled bookcases placed closely face to face and drawn out into a gangway to give access to the shelves (Fig. 57). Another derived its nature from the practice of arranging the smaller sizes of book in double rows on a shelf to save space. Inconvenience inevitably arose when books in the rear rows were required, to avoid which, it was suggested separate shelves might be used for the two 'layers,' the books in the front being easily swung aside on their shelves when it was desired to reach those in the rear. In an experiment conducted on these lines at Bradford between 1878 and 1884 by the City Librarian, Charles G. Virgo, equipment was introduced which foreshadowed very closely the hinged shelving for compact storage now in use in the United States. It consisted of a press, hinged at one side and mounted in front of fixed shelving, access to which was obtained by opening the hinged press in the manner of a door. The equipment was constructed of wood, and to give additional support to the hinged press a roller was attached to the outer edge, running on a curved metal track in the floor. Shelving of this pattern remained in use at Bradford until at least 1903, but was apparently later dismantled, and as there is no record of any having been introduced elsewhere, it may not have been entirely successful: perhaps some weakness resulted from its wooden construction.

The Copyright Libraries, above all, were confronted during the latter half of the nineteenth century with a vast increase in the rate of accessions, and consequently augmented demands on the storage space available. In one of his essays[1] Richard Garnett describes early experiments in providing additional shelf-room in libraries, and after brief references to equipment at Trinity College, Dublin, and the Bodleian, he relates how the problem of congestion had occupied the attention of the authorities at the British Museum and how, visiting the public library at Bethnal Green during 1886, he realized the suitability of movable presses there to meet the needs of the Museum. Fortunately for the Museum authorities the stacks of the Iron Library, with wide gangways and grated iron floors, lent themselves admirably to the installation of additional movable presses. One form introduced was double-sided, of the same size as the fixed wall presses, and suspended from rails bolted to the cast-iron stack supports above (Fig. 55). The books on the front shelves of the sliding press, as it came to be called in the Museum, were accessible without its being moved, while it could be drawn out into the centre of the gangway to give access to the books in its rear shelves and to those on the fixed shelves behind. Another type, used in the narrow galleries of the Iron Library, ran sideways on rails in front of the fixed presses but was less capacious, since it held only a single layer of books; moreover, to permit move-

1. 'The Sliding Press at the British Museum', in *The Library*, Oct. 1891, ser. I, vol. 3, pp. 414-20. Reprinted in *Essays in Librarianship and Bibliography*, 1899.

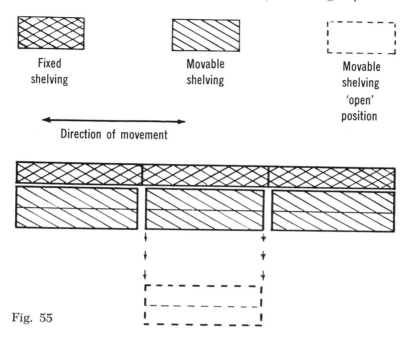

Fixed
shelving

Movable
shelving

Movable
shelving
'open'
position

Direction of movement

Fig. 55

ment sideways presses of this type were fitted only in front of alternate fixed presses, although it would in some cases have been possible to introduce a higher proportion (Fig. 56). The equipment was cheap to manufacture and easy to install, and since presses could be added singly as required at almost any part of the library, some sections of which became congested more rapidly than others, it was of very great value in enabling accessions to be housed without large-scale rearrangement of the books or extension of the building.

Sliding presses remained in use at the British Museum for many years and proved perfectly satisfactory, provided that care was taken to replace books correctly to avoid the risk of

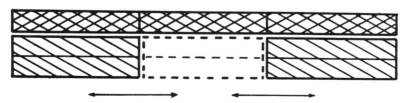

Fig. 56

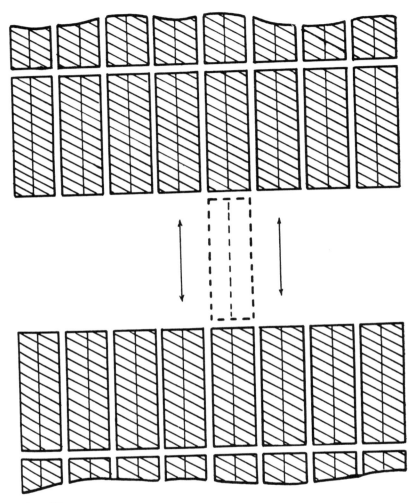

Fig. 57

damage from the movement of the press. As long as the running
gear was well lubricated the weight of the presses, even when
full, caused no difficulty in operation, but the total load which
they imposed on the cast-iron structure in excess of that for
which it was designed led to their removal about 1920, and made
necessary the reconstruction of the Iron Library. The only other
movable shelving in the British Museum was added in 1931,
when two lofty rooms were converted into stacks by inserting
intermediate floors. In this type of press (Fig. 57) shelves were

attached to each side of steel frames 7 ft. high and 3 ft. 7 in. wide, suspended from rollers running in a framework of steel girders at ceiling level. To gain the maximum economy in space, the presses, which were fitted with 7½-in. shelving, were hung as close together as possible, having to be drawn out sideways into the gangway before a book could be removed. Here again, however, there proved to be a risk of damage to books, and coupled with it a danger of books on partly filled shelves being dislodged by the movement of the press.

The problem of congestion has continued into our own times, thanks to the perpetual increase in the rate of expansion of library stocks and the ever-rising costs of building and equipment. The librarian whose shelves are full and who cannot make space by discarding outdated and unwanted material has various courses of action open to him. He may obtain additional shelving of conventional pattern, or make use of microcopy—methods lying beyond the scope of this paper, though it is worth noting that the cost of converting newspapers into microfilm has been estimated to be higher than that of providing the bare essentials for satisfactory storage of the originals.[2] An alternative solution, however, is to increase the capacity of an existing building by the more effective use of ordinary shelving or the introduction of shelving specially designed for compact storage.

One of the leading advocates of compact storage using conventional fixed shelving is Fremont Rider, whose methods are described in his *Compact book storage*,[3] a work based on his experience as librarian of Wesleyan University, Middletown, Connecticut. Pointing out that detailed attention has been paid in recent years to the cost of cataloguing books, but little to that of housing them, he comments on the rapid growth of libraries which, in the light of constantly rising building and maintenance costs, makes the efficient use of storage essential. In the usual American library building, Rider continues, aisles occupy 65 per cent of the total volume and shelves 35 per cent. On shelves where room is left for the addition of accessions in classified order, an average of 35 per cent is occupied by books. In such conditions, only 10 per cent of the total available space is effectively used, and an improvement of 10 per cent in efficiency

2. Esterquest, Ralph T., 'New directions in condensed book storage', in *Review of Documentation*, vol. 18, fasc. I, pp. 29, 30. (FID XVIIIth Conference, 1951.)
3. Rider, Fremont, *Compact book storage*, p. 90. Hadham Press, New York, 1949.

would double the storage capacity. To use 100 per cent of the space would be to reduce accessibility to nil, and the solution lies in striking a satisfactory balance between capacity and availability.

Rider's proposals require no special shelving, though they can well be applied to shelving manufactured to provide compact storage. Arranging books by sizes, he estimates, achieves an economy in space of 25 per cent: much depends on whether classified arrangement is used in stacks, and if so, to what extent detailed subdivision is carried out. The examination of 100,000 volumes in the library of Brown University led to the following conclusions:

Height of volumes	Proportion of total
Under 20 cm. (7⅞ in.)	Over 28 per cent
20–23 cm. (7⅞–9 in.)	Over 31 per cent
23–25 cm. (9–9⅞ in.)	Over 21 per cent
25–28 cm. (9⅞–11 in.)	Over 10 per cent

Thus over 90 per cent of the contents of the library fell into these size groups and were suitable for close shelving by size. Proportions vary greatly in different subjects: at Yale the proportion of octavo volumes varied from 45½ per cent in works on art to 96 per cent in those on history and literature.

Rider aimed at a saving of 50 per cent, and as one step towards this end he resorted to shelving books with the fore-edge down. Location marks were written in Indian ink on the lower edge, which was trimmed smooth for the purpose when necessary. Some little-used material—that unlikely to be required more than once in two years—was shelved in cardboard boxes, which were found to be very convenient for the purpose and cost only one-tenth as much as binding. Six standard sizes of box were used, and material shelved in this way included publications in need of binding but not worth the expense, small books and those so thin that the shelfmark could not be written on the lower edge, cuttings, maps, manuscript material, sheet music, &c. A small number of works such as government publications of minor importance were prepared more drastically for shelving by having the margins and with them the edges of the boards cut down in the guillotine to reduce the size of the book.

Though other libraries have been obliged to adopt these or similar measures, Fremont Rider alone has recorded the results in detail. As an alternative, or to supplement such methods, it may be decided to provide increased shelf space without altering

the total volume of a stack building. Where all shelving is to remain stationary, the means adopted is the reduction of the width
of aisles and gangways, where stack design allows, sacrificing in
consequence some comfort in working conditions. Robert H.
Muller[1] quotes the case of Southern Illinois University, which has
a stack with 18-in. circular columns spaced at 23-ft. intervals. Between columns five double-faced ranges of shelving had been installed, giving, with 8-in. shelving, aisles of 38.7 in. width. In an
experiment, progressive reduction of aisle widths gave increases
of up to 40 per cent in capacity, this figure being reached with
22.9-in. aisles. The widths tested had to be chosen to avoid block-
ing of aisles by the stack columns. The 22.9-in. aisles were pro-
nounced extremely uncomfortable by the staff using them, but
much depends on the type of material stored under such conditions and the frequency with which it is required for use. At Yale
the staff found 22-in. aisles satisfactory for little-used material.
Remington Rand, by reducing aisles to 20 in. and lowering the
number of transverse gangways, claim to have obtained an increase of 69 per cent in stack capacity. This is done by using the
'four-way bookstack' introduced by Remington Rand, which is
formed from a 'chassis' or self-contained framework, having uprights to which the shelves are attached. The distance between
the uprights is 4 ft. 4 in. in one direction and 3 ft. in the other,
and the shelving may run in either direction, giving, with 8-in.
shelving, alternative aisle widths of 3 ft. and 1 ft. 8 in. The chassis
may be moved if it is desired to alter the arrangement of shelving,
and can be used, singly or in numbers, in workrooms or other
parts of a library in addition to the stack proper. This is the only
compact storage equipment at present available in which all the
shelves remain stationary in use. Other types depend on moving
shelves or drawers to make material available, some being designed as free-standing units which may be used in conjunction
with fixed shelving or independently, others for attachment to
fixed shelving.

The Vernier mobile bookstack made by Messrs. Libraco of
Charlton, London, S.E. 7, is a free-standing double-sided press
mounted on casters with specially designed roller bearings, which,
the makers claim, ensure that it does not 'wander' in use (Fig.
57). This equipment dispenses with the rail or running surface

4. 'Evaluation of compact book storage systems', in *The Third Library
Building Plans Institute, conducted by the Association of College and
Reference Libraries Buildings Committee.* Chicago, 1954. [ACRL Mon-
ographs, No. 11.]

necessary with some kinds of movable shelving, which must be attached to or sunk into the floor, or suspended from overhead, involving additional work and expense in installation, and hindering any subsequent alteration in the layout of the shelving. Those with experience state that provided the floor on which the book-stack stands is hard and perfectly level, no difficulties arise in using it. An installation of 158 presses in the Mitchell Library, Glasgow, arranged in double columns with the presses standing face to face, with gangways of sufficient width to enable any press to be fully withdrawn, and with fixed shelving applied to the surrounding walls, accommodates 81,000 volumes in an area of 2,100 sq. ft., where only 44,640 volumes could be housed in fixing shelving. Any volume may be reached with only one press movement.

Shelving recently supplied by the firm of J. Glover & Sons, Ltd., of Groton Road, London, S.W. 18, for installation in the Royal Library at Stockholm and Uppsala University Library is that known as the 'Stormor' type, and resembles the sliding press designed for use in the galleries of the Iron Library at the British Museum, being single-sided and moving sideways on rails to give access to fixed shelving, or further movable shelving, in the rear (Fig. 56). At Stockholm up to five 'layers' of movable shelving were installed in front of fixed presses, in bays of a maximum breadth of 36 ft. In one room thus equipped an increase of 176 per cent in storage capacity was claimed, and in another, 101 per cent. The presses, which were designed for the flat storage of unbound newspapers, had shelves of 2 ft. 6 in. $\times$ 1 ft. 6 in. or 2 ft. $\times$ 1 ft. 3 in., spaced at 4-in. vertical intervals. Messrs. Acrow (Engineers) Ltd., of South Wharf, London, W. 2, make a similar type of shelving, which has been installed in the Aberdeen, Paddington, and Hornsey Public Libraries and the John Rylands Library.

Of the types of compact storage shelving designed for use independently of fixed shelving, one, derived from industrial storage equipment, is that known as the Compactus system, the Foulkes Mobile Storage system, or the Compactus-Ingold system, which is the invention of a Swiss engineer, and is manufactured in Great Britain by Messrs. Glover (Fig. 58). A unique feature is the use of electric power to move the shelving. Bays of double-sided presses may be up to 23 ft. wide; the bays are arranged in columns, face to face, having in each column a vacant space the width of a gangway. The bays move on rails laid in the direction of the length of the column, and midway between the rails is an open channel sunk into the floor. In this channel runs an endless

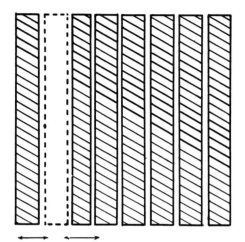

Fig. 58

steel rope, kept in motion while the shelving is in use by an electric motor, normally of ¼ h.p. At the ends of each bay are levers,
operation of any of which causes the cable to be gripped by jaws
below the centre of the bay concerned; in this way the bays are
moved to and fro, and a gangway opened at the desired point in
the column. The effect may be compared to the pushing aside of
volumes on a partly filled bookshelf to open a space, the space being needed in this instance so that the operator may enter and
have access to the shelves. When the lever is moved in the opposite direction, the movement of the bays is reversed. Gangways
can be opened at more than one point in the column simultaneously, if sufficient space is left in designing the installation, and
as the grip on the cable is not a positive one, the movement of
the bays, which is at the rate of 30 ft. per minute, can be checked
by the hand, so that there is no danger of a person at the shelves
being crushed by someone else wishing to have access at another
point. When the bays are closed, dust and dirt are excluded by
rubber beading round the edges, and there is a good measure of
protection against fire. The economy afforded by the use of this
system is shown by its introduction into the offices of the 'Patria'
Insurance Society at Basle,[5] the offices of which are in the centre
of the city, where land is very expensive. Additional space was
required for records, and, as the building was suitable, Compactus equipment was installed. An estimate of the cost of rebuilding to provide an additional 660 cu. m. of space was 72,600

5. Kaiser, L., 'Ein neues Regalsystem', in *Nachrichten f. wiss. Bibliotheken*,
   Jahrg. 6, Hft. ¾, Mai 1953.

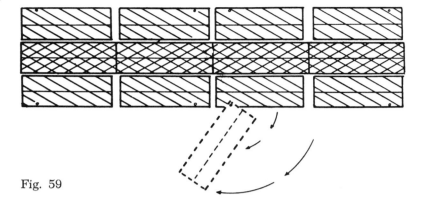

Fig. 59

fr., whereas the Compactus installation, giving the same amount of storage by effecting an increase of 115 per cent in the capacity of the existing premises, cost 15,000 fr., a saving of 57,600 fr., or approximately 79 per cent.

Compact storage is already employed in the United States, and among the types of movable shelving designed for use in conjunction with fixed presses is that manufactured by Messrs. Snead & Co., of Orange, Va., one of the earliest installations of which is to be found in the Midwest Inter-Library Center, Chicago (Fig. 59). The Snead system makes use of fixed and movable shelves, and takes the form of a triple bank of double-sided adjustable steel shelving, the centre presses being fixed and each having a double-sided press of the same width hinged to each face. There are thus six layers of shelves between stack aisles, and each outer compartment can be swung open like a door to afford access to books on its inner side and on the fixed centre shelving—a modern application of the principle introduced by Virgo at Bradford. The swinging motion of the outer compartments is controlled rigidly, the makers claim, without the use of rails or guides, so that the shelves cannot sway or wobble, and as the presses are hinged on ball-bearings, little effort is needed to open them. In the Midwest Inter-Library Center the aisles are 3 ft. 4 in. wide; the presses in opening move through more than 90°, so that when one is fully open the shelving projects 1 ft. 4 in. into the aisle, still leaving sufficient room to pass. Where a greater degree of economy is necessary, a second hinged press, opening in the opposite direction to the first, can be fitted in front of it. The makers estimate that with one double-sided press fitted

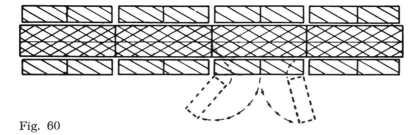

Fig. 60

on each face of fixed presses there is an economy, where 8-in. shelving is used, of 66 per cent over fixed shelving 4 ft. 4 in. between centres (3 ft.-aisle), and 44 per cent even when the aisles are reduced to 2 ft. 5 in. Material on the inner shelves is protected from dirt and to some extent from fire, and the hinged presses can be locked in position.

A similar type of shelving is made by the Art Metal Company of Jamestown, N.Y., being known as the Com-Pac-Case Storage System (Fig. 60). This may be adopted for new installations, or applied to existing fixed shelving, where conditions permit. Unlike the Snead equipment, the Com-Pac-Case movable presses are single-sided; the standard pattern is 7 ft. 2 in. high and has adjustable shelves 9 in. deep and 15 in. wide. Units are hinged to each side of the front of fixed presses 3 ft. wide; a space of 3¼ in. between the inner sides of the hinged units permits one-half to be opened without disturbing the other. The hinged units are secured in the closed position by a spring-loaded bolt and may be fastened with a padlock. When the equipment is incorporated in a new installation, it is normally applied to each face of fixed shelving, while additional fixed shelves are placed across the ends of bays. The shelves of the hinged units of standard pattern face outwards, but if required units may be manufactured with shelves which face inwards, giving greater protection to the material contained at the cost of immediate availability. As with the Snead equipment, two rows of hinged units may be fitted in front of each face of fixed shelving, where conditions permit. The distance between the centres of bays recommended by the manufacturers is 4 ft. 6 in. when a single layer of hinged presses is added to fixed shelving, to be increased to 6 ft. when two layers of movable shelving are used. The gangways between bays, when the hinged presses are closed, are approximately 1 ft. 9 in. and 1 ft. 11 in. respectively, which does not allow room for passing when the hinged presses are open.

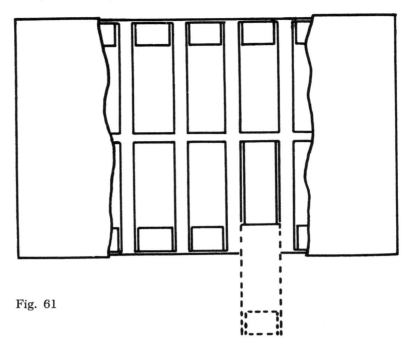

Fig. 61

The weight of hinged presses does not call for undue effort in their use. Fearing that this might be the case, Rider suggested that individual shelves could be hinged and independently movable—a suggestion which does not seem to have commended itself to manufacturers as yet, doubtless because of the greater costs and complexity which would result.

In the Hamilton Compo stack equipment, which is now being made in the United States, drawers take the place of shelves, and a 'floating slide' permits any drawer to be opened to its fullest extent without becoming dislodged (Fig. 61). Books may be placed upright or fore-edge down, one row across the front of the drawer and an additional row along each side. Those in the front may be removed without opening the drawer. The drawers are 18 in., 22 in., or 26 in. in width, and up to 48 in. in length. The uprights to which the slides are attached are slotted and permit vertical adjustment of drawers to suit the size of books being housed. Single drawers or entire compartments may be fitted with locks. The manufacturers, the Hamilton Manufacturing Co., of Two Rivers, Wisconsin, claim that increases of up to 100 per cent in storage capacity can be obtained with their equipment; the only criticism of which, in the absence of first-hand experience, is that the identification and removal of books in the higher drawers might be difficult, particularly if they were placed fore-edge down.

The Stor-Mor equipment made by the W. R. Ames Co., of San Francisco, employs double-headed drawers, designed to give 100 per cent increase in capacity with no decrease in the width of aisles. In the Charles Holbrook Library of the Pacific School of Religion at Berkeley, Cal., an increase of 113 per cent was claimed to have been achieved through the introduction of Stor-Mor equipment. Like the Hamilton drawers these may be installed in existing library buildings; unlike them they have no shelf fitted across the front of the drawer and directly accessible, but books are shelved in two rows along the length of the drawer, fore-edge inward. The drawer assembly is such that it may be mounted on stack supports designed for fixed bracket-type shelving, and the two sizes of drawer advertised measure 16% in. wide and 68% or 76% in. long. Other sizes are available. Two drawers side by side have the same width as a standard 3-ft. shelf. The height of the front of the drawers is 7% in.; to permit the removal of books there are no raised sides, while supports are fitted to hold books in place when the drawers are moved. The length of the drawers is such that when fixed shelving is replaced by Stor-Mor equipment, as with Hamilton, the space formerly occupied by alternate aisles is made available for books. The drawers run on ball-bearing rollers, will open with a pull of less than 3 lb., and are held in place when closed by a locking catch. They are fitted with two 5 × 3 in. card holders at each end to enable the contents to be indicated. The makers state that all volumes are easily visible when the drawers are open. The equipment is in use in Stanford University Library, and is to be installed in the libraries of California and Michigan Universities.

During the last century the number of libraries in which compact storage equipment was used remained very small, and, conditions varying in each, it was often necessary to make special equipment for an individual library. Now, with the designing of library buildings capable of receiving fixed shelving of standard pattern, and the introduction, especially in the United States, of the principle of modular construction in which the interior of a building is constructed in units of uniform size so that their conversion from one use to another, e.g. from workroom to stack, is rendered comparatively simple and inexpensive, the manufacture and installation of compact storage equipment has become practicable, and most types are in fact suitable for introduction into stacks originally designed for fixed shelving, though they can also be effectively employed in other locations. Again, the adoption of artificial lighting and ventilation for library stacks, so that no difficulty arises over the obstruction of light or air when shelving arrangements are altered, greatly facilitates the use of compact storage equipment. It seems doubtful, however, whether compact shelving can be satisfactorily introduced into parts of a library to which readers have unrestricted access, though the Hamilton Company affirm that no difficulty is likely to be encountered and that they have in fact received orders for equipment to be used in such conditions.

In assessing the suitability of compact storage equipment for any particular library, it must be remembered that material thus stored is not as readily available as that on fixed shelving. In the Snead equipment, for example, the proportion available without any shelf movement is one-third or one-fifth, and in the Art Metal, one-half or none, according to the design. With the Libraco Vernier and Compactus shelving on the other hand, a shelf movement is necessary whenever it is desired to remove or replace material. Compact storage is accordingly most profitably used for material in little demand. In experiments carried out at the Midwest Inter-Library Center, forty journeys to the stack were made, a check being kept on the time required to remove and to reshelve books. It was concluded that 8½ seconds more were required to remove a book from the inner sections of Snead hinged shelving than from fixed shelving, and 10½ seconds more to replace it. When related to the time needed to reach the stack floor by lift and walk normal stack distances, the report of the experiment concluded, the additional time involved was found to be somewhat under 10 per cent.

The initial cost of compact storage equipment is high, and the only justification for its use is the achievement of an ultimate economy, in calculating which consideration must be given to the cost of equipment, the extent to which space is saved, the cost of building construction, and that of future maintenance. Much depends on the circumstances of individual cases, and it has not proved practicable to estimate the average cost of stack construction in this country at the present time. Again, sufficient evidence has not accumulated for any reliable forecast of maintenance costs to be made. Maintenance and repair of compact storage equipment will obviously be higher than that of fixed shelving, particularly as the age of an installation increases. It is reported from the Midwest Inter-Library Center that as yet no signs of wear in the shelving have become apparent.

The following table, which assumes an arbitrary price for stack construction of £3 per sq. ft. of floor space, excluding the cost of land, is intended to give an idea of the relative saving in space and cost of two types of movable shelving, but the figures should be regarded with caution, since very much depends on the particular nature of any installation.

Fixed Shelving (Libraco): £39. 10s. per press of 7 4ft. shelves (double sided) giving 56 ft. run of shelf.

Cost per ft. run . . . . . . 14s. 1d.
Floor area required per ft. run° . . . 0.308 sq. ft.
Cost of shelving and building per ft. run of shelf £1. 12s. 6½d.

Libraco Vernier movable shelving: £49. 10s. per press of 56 ft. run of shelf.

Cost per ft. run . . . . . . 17s. 8d.
Floor area required per ft. run° . . . . 0.195 sq. ft.
Cost of shelving and building per ft. run of shelving £1. 9s. 4½d.

Glover 'Compactus' equipment. Quotation for a specimen installation having 5 presses per 15 ft. bay, each press having 7 3ft. shelves, 210 ft. run of shelf per bay, and 10 bays per column.

	s.	d.
Cost of shelving per ft. run	5	3
Cost of wheeled base and rope-gripping device, &c.		
£46. 2s. 11d., or per ft. run of shelving .	4	8
Cost of track, wire rope, &c., per ft. run of shelving		3
Cost of motor per ft. run of shelving		3
	10	5

Floor area required per ft. run of shelving°° 0.101 sq. ft.
Cost of shelving and building per ft. run of shelving 16s. 6d.

°Including aisle and proportion of main gangway.
°°Including proportion of gangway.

Where only a few bays of moderate weight are to be used, hand operation is practicable, with consequent reduction in installation and maintenance costs. The cost of installation, which has not been included in the above figures, may be estimated at 15 per cent of that of the equipment, but much depends on the nature of the existing floors on which it is to be fitted. The cost of operation is negligible as small h.p. motors are used, e.g. ¼ h.p. to move loads of up to 15 tons, and it is only necessary for the power to be switched on when movement is desired, unless the installation is in continuous use. Maintenance of motors and other moving equipment would, of course, have to be taken into consideration.

Muller, in a similar comparison of American equipment, gives the cost of shelving (excluding building costs) per volume as follows:

	$
Fixed shelving	0.16
Hamilton drawers	0.54
Ames 'Stor-Mor' drawers	0.57
Art Metal hinged units:	
two units per face of fixed shelving . . .	0.56
four units (double layer on each face) . . .	0.65

The variation in cost between the different types of American compact storage equipment was surprisingly small.

The extensive use of compact storage equipment is therefore economically justifiable when building costs are very high, when land values are high and vertical extension impossible, or when for any reason extension or rebuilding is completely impossible. As a temporary expedient to provide relief in particularly congested sections of a library, its value has already been shown. As the cost of building rises, so compact shelving, which makes a smaller building possible, becomes more profitable to use. The initial cost of a storehouse building remote from the library it serves may well be far less than that of any extension or installation of compact storage equipment in a building in urban surroundings, but the recurring cost of transport, additional labour, maintenance of the building, and the inavailability of material may make it a doubtful bargain. An additional factor encountered in the United States more than in European countries is the cost of installing and operating air-conditioning apparatus. Muller calculated that, using the Hamilton equipment, no financial gain whatever was achieved where the basic cost of a building was less than $12.50 per sq. ft. At $15 per sq. ft. the gam was 8.9 per cent, rising to 18.6 per cent at $20 and 29 per cent at $30. Economies would have been shown at an earlier point if the cost of land, power, and heating had been considered.

To sum up, the advantages of compact storage methods are: a saving in building, lighting, heating, and ventilation installations and running costs, in floor covering and maintenance, in staff time in reaching the shelves from the service point, and in cleaning and decoration. Against this, the principal disadvantages are the cost of equipment and the fact that books are less directly accessible. Equipment must be maintained, and may cause noise, the removal and replacement of books requires more time, aisles may be obstructed by drawers or swinging shelves, and the admission of readers into compact storage sections may lead to difficulties or even accidents. There is a danger of books being damaged by the movement of shelves or drawers, particularly if they have not been replaced correctly on the shelves. When compact storage is introduced into existing buildings, the floors must be sufficiently strong (normal stack construction allows an adequate margin), and provision for lighting, ventilation, and access must remain unobstructed or else undergo modification. Much depends on the conditions and requirements of the individual case, and the final economy likely to result—if indeed an economy is to be obtained through the use of compact storage—is only to be assessed by a detailed analysis of every aspect of the costs involved, both at the time of installation and throughout the useful life of the equipment.[6]

I am very much obliged to the numerous manufacturers and librarians who have kindly supplied information for inclusion in this paper. I am particularly grateful to Mr. Robert H. Muller and to the Association of College and Research Libraries for permission to quote from Mr. Muller's articles on compact storage.

6. Muller, 'Compact storage equipment: where to use it and where not,' in *College and Research Libraries,* vol. 15, no. 3 (1954), pp. 300-308.

Evaluation of Compact Book Storage Systems[1]

Robert H. Muller

Perhaps the chief reason for the interest of librarians in compact book stacks is their desire to reduce the cost of storing books in libraries. Only if it can be shown that it is much cheaper to store books firmly packed than to store them in a more porous or dispersed fashion, *all factors considered*, will librarians resort to compact storage for certain less frequently used types of books and documents that must be kept in the main building.

In analyzing book storage cost, we must take account of three factors: (1) The cost of the compact stack equipment, (2) the degree of compactness in book storage achieved through the equipment, and (3) the building construction cost. We shall briefly consider each of these variables and then comment on their relations to each other. Our analysis will be confined to three types of compact storage equipment that are available on the current market and have been displayed at library conferences, to wit, those manufactured by (a) the W. R. Ames Company, San Francisco, California, (b) the Art Metal Manufacturing Company, Jamestown, New York, and (c) the Hamilton Manufacturing Company, Two Rivers, Wisconsin. In addition, we shall analyze the compact storage plan most recently advocated by (d) Remington Rand Inc., New York. However, our

1. The author gratefully acknowledges his debt to: (1) Mr. Reider B. Jacobsen, of Architectural Services of Southern Illinois University, for preparing the drawings; (2) Miss Grace E. Kite, of Southern Illinois University Libraries, for aiding the author in preliminary comparative studies of compact storage equipment; (3) the W. R. Ames Company, the Art Metal Construction Company, the Hamilton Manufacturing Company, and Remington Rand, Incorporated, for making their equipment available for purposes of study, and their respective representatives, Mr. V. H. Gallichotte, Mr. F. Beaumont, Mr. Clifford S. Brown, and Mr. Scott Cherry, for their cooperation and interest; (4) Jerrold Orne, Director of Libraries of Air University, Maxwell Air Force Base, Alabama, and Ferris S. Randall, Assistant Director of Libraries for Technical Services for constructive suggestions after reading the manuscript.

discussion will be primarily concerned with free-standing stack equipment; it will only incidentally touch upon the claims made for converting a self-supporting multiple-tier stack into a more compact stack, as was recently done in the Yale University Libraries by Remington Rand through the use of four-way book stack columns, involving the setting of double-faced ranges with 10-inch shelves 42 inches center to center and allowing only 22 inches for aisle space.[2] Also omitted from our discussion will be the methods of compact storage advocated by Fremont Rider, involving the sizing and shelving of books with their short edges presented to the aisle, since these methods can be used, although perhaps not with equal success, either with adjustable bracket type shelving or with adjustable compact storage equipment, and thus represent additional increases in storage capacity of alleged-ly 50 per cent or more, applicable to all adjustable types of shelving.[3]

Two other manufacturers, the Globe Wernicke Company, Cincinnati, Ohio, and the Virginia Metal Products Company, Orange, Va., were reported to have prepared designs for compact book storage but were not ready to discuss their plans, as of February, 1954. An earlier type of compact storage, involving hinged units on casters and manufactured by Snead and Company, Orange, Va., was installed in the Midwest Inter-Library Center,[4] but is apparently no longer in production.

Although experimentation with compact book storage can be traced to the early nineties of the 19th century,[5] the development and promotion of new designs has apparently received new impetus since the widespread adoption of "modular" design for library buildings and the concomitant gradual abandonment of the conventional multi-tier self-supporting stack involving narrow fixed column spacing.

Equipment Cost. In order to compare the cost of different types of free-standing compact stacks, we obtained informal

---

2. John H. Ottemiller, "Yale Divinity Library Creates Shelf Space with Pioneer Plan," *Pioneer* (Library Bureau Div., Remington Rand Inc.), 16: 6-8 (Nov.-Dec. 1953). See also: Yale Medical Library. *Annual Report*, 30 June 1952, pp. 7-11.

3. Fremont Rider, *Compact Book Storage* (New York: Hadham Press, 1949), pp. 37, 57.

4. Ralph T. Esterquest, "New Directions in Condensed Book Storage," *Review of Documentation* (F.I.D.) 18: 29-30 (March, 1951). See also: "Snead System of Compact Storage" (advertisement), *Wilson Library Bulletin*, 25: 207 (Nov., 1950).

5. Rider, *op. cit.*, p. 30.

Table 1

Cost Comparisons: Compact and Conventional Stacks

Shelving, 7 rows high	Linear feet per unit	Volumes per unit	Cost per unit	Cost per volume
Hamilton, 18 inches wide, 3 feet deep drawers	40.4	242	$130.09	$ .54
Art Metal, 4 swing units, 8 inch shelves	78.4	472	265.00	.56
Art Metal, 8 swing units, 8 inch shelves	119.0	714	462.00	.65
Ames	155.5	896	508.44	.57
Conventional bracket type, free-standing, 8 inch shelves, double-sections	41.1	247	39.52	.16

quantity quotations from the manufacturers early in 1954.[6] We then converted the quotations into per-volume cost figures, assuming that 6 volumes per linear foot represented practical working capacity.[7] Table 1 shows the figures for the units compared with bracket type conventional shelving, completely erected.

6. The quotations from the W. R. Ames Company applied to 1340 Stor-Mor drawers (type B-500), installed. The quotations from the Art Metal Company applied to a double-faced bay of bracket type shelving, 36 inches wide by 90 inches high, containing 7 shelves on each side, together with either 4 or 8 swing units, two on each side, all shelves of 8-inch actual depth, erected complete; approximately 10% was added to the prices to take care of price changes for various parts of the country, due to variations in labor and transportation costs, as well as job conditions. The quotations from the Hamilton Manufacturing Company were for Compo stacks, completely installed and including all necessary accessories, usable with 8 rows of shelves although the prices shown in the tabulation apply to an installation actually using only 7 rows of shelves; the accessories include range indicators, book supports, one for each shelf, as well as book supports and shelf support extensions for oversize books. The quotations for bracket-type conventional shelving were supplied by Remington Rand, Incorporated, applicable to 30 foot ranges, stack columns 7 feet 6 inches high, 7 rows of shelves, delivered and installed in the Eastern region. All companies permitted publication of their approximate quotation.
7. J. L. Wheeler and A. M. Githens, *The American Public Library Building* (Chicago: American Library Association, 1941), p. 414.

The per-volume cost of the least expensive type of compact book storage system was over three times, and the most expensive four times, as high as the cost of adjustable steel bracket type shelving. Cost differences on a per-volume basis between the products of the three manufacturers were fairly small, which would indicate that compact storage equipment costs are probably controlled by competitive bidding to a considerable extent and by certain inescapable fixed costs for metal and fabrication.

Compactness. Let us now ask whether the available compact storage systems really increase the book holding capacity sufficiently to warrant the extra cost per volume and whether, in this respect, there are significant differences between the various systems. This analysis is based on layout drawings for each of the systems for a floor area measuring 23 by 23 feet from center to center of 18-inch-wide, round columns, which represented the dimensions for a typical bay in the new library building of Southern Illinois University. No claim is made that our calculations would apply precisely to areas of different sizes; but the general relationships will probably be approximately the same for other dimensions.

Into a bay measuring 23 by 23 feet could be placed 5 double-faced ranges (actually 4 double-faced plus 2 single-faced ranges) on 55.2 inch centers,[8] each range consisting of 7 standard 3-foot double-faced sections.

Let us first look at the proposal to increase storage capacity by narrowing the range aisles in a double bay, but all other conditions remaining equal.

Table 2 shows the percentage gains over the conventional range spacing for the following aisle widths, assuming 8-inch shelves: 33.7 inches (Plan B), 29.5 inches (Plan C), 26.0 inches (Plan D), and 22.9 inches (Plan E). Plan A provided the conventional arrangement. Under Plan B, we managed to squeeze one additional double range into a double bay, but had to eliminate 2 double sections near each of the center columns in order to permit access to two of the range aisles that would otherwise have been blocked by the columns and reduced openings to about 12 inches; the percentage gain of storage capacity was, therefore, relatively small under this plan. The same held true for Plan D where the columns also interfered. Hence the only

8. For current American standards, see: William H. Jesse, *Shelf Work* (Chicago: American Library Association, 1952), p. 39; Jesse recommends a spacing of 52 or 54 inches center to center.

Table 2

*Capacity Increases Through Aisle Reduction
with Conventional Stacks*

Plan	Approx. aisle width (8 inch shelves), in inches	Center to center distance of ranges, in inches	No. of double sections per double bay	No. of double ranges added per double bay	No. of aisles between alternate columns	Percentage gain of storage capacity
A	38.7	55.2	70	—	10	—
B	33.7	50.2	73	3/7	11	4.3
C	29.5	46.0	84	2	12	20.0
D	26.0	42.5	87	2-3/7	13	24.3
E	22.9	39.4	98	4	14	40.0

feasible storage plans seemed to be Plans C and E, involving aisle widths of 29.5 inches and 22.9 inches, respectively.

At this point individual judgment enters into the picture: If you regard 22.9 inches as adequate for an aisle width in storage stacks, Plan E will be your choice. At Southern Illinois University, we have experimented with 22-inch aisles and have found them exceedingly uncomfortable. It all depends, however, on the type of material shelved in such stacks. Associate Librarian John H. Ottemiller, of Yale University, wrote to me in November 1953 as follows: "Please understand our librarians here are quite satisfied with 22 inch aisles; they work. We fully realize, however, that 22 inches is a narrow space for heavily used sections of books. In other words, it is not comfortable to work in the aisles for an extended period of time examining books on shelves." The so-called "Wesleyan" book truck, developed by Fremont Rider and manufactured by Remington Rand, may make narrow aisles of not less than about 22 inches, a little less inconvenient to use; the truck, which is slightly less than 19 inches wide, plus 3 inches clearance for wheel turning, and a little over 29 inches long, provides tilted shelves on the narrow sides of the truck. Such a truck costs approximately $165.00 on single orders.

Fremont Rider reported that Melvil Dewey "advocated 30 inches as a minimum; he would permit 26 inches, in the clear, in the extreme emergency—which goes a good deal narrower than most of us would."[9] The claim made by Remington Rand in a recent advertisement[10]—"Now Library Bureau gives you 69% more storage in the same space!"—is true only if you assume a relatively comfortable stack arrangement before the change and an exceedingly uncomfortable one (20 inch aisles with 8-inch shelves and no cross aisles for ranges of 8 continuous 3 foot sections) after the change. In our studies we assumed identical conditions before and after the change as far as cross aisles were concerned and were unable to calculate a higher gain than 40 per cent with range aisles 22.9 inches in the clear for 8-inch shelves, which should take care of 89 per cent of the books in a typical university library, leaving the remaining 11 per cent for oversize shelving.[11]

We included the aisle reduction plans in the tabulations showing the gain in storage capacity achieved through different compact storage methods. Table 3, which compares capacity increases of different plans, indicates the greatest gain for Hamilton (109.3%) and the smallest one for the moderate aisle reduction plan (20%). In compactness, the 7 storage methods varied considerably from one another.

Several comments on the layout drawings that formed the basis for the foregoing tabulations may be in order: (1) The data showing the number of volumes represented theoretical maximum capacities, without provision for cross aisles or main aisles; such maximum capacities seemed more reliable for purposes of comparison than practically tolerable capacities because maxima could be determined independent of subjective judgment as to the most desirable spacing of cross aisles. (2) An effort was made to stay strictly within the bounds of a single 23 by 23 foot bay as far as placing and operating the equipment was concerned; this limitation resulted in a small amount of wasted floor area for all systems except Ames. (3) An exception to this rule had to be made in the case of the relatively bulky Ames units; otherwise the Ames equipment layout would have shown a substantially lower capacity increase, which would have been unfair to the W. R. Ames Company; the drawing showing

9. Rider, *op. cit.*, p. 40.
10. *College and Research Libraries*, V, 14: inside cover following page 112 (Jan., 1953). See also the advertising folder entitled, "Remington Rand's New Compact Storage Stacks Are Flexible and Convertible," distributed in 1953/54.
11. Rider, *op cit.*, p. 45. Incidentally, an 8-inch shelf, as usually defined, is actually only 7 inches deep, but accommodates books that are 8 inches wide.

Table 3

Capacity Increases for Different Compact Storage Plans

	Range aisles (inches)	No. of units per bay (maximum)	No. of linear ft. per unit	No. of vol. per unit	No. of vol. per bay	Gain over conventional shelving	Percentage gain
Conventional shelving 8″ shelves	38.7	35	41.1	247	8,645	—	—
Aisle reduction plan, moderate, 8″ shelves	29.5	42	41.1	247	10,374	1,729	20.0
Aisle reduction plan, severe, 8″ shelves	22.9	49	41.1	247	12,103	3,458	40.0
Art Metal, 4 swing units, 8″ shelves (Fig. 62)	28.5	28	78.4	472	13,216	4,571	52.9
Art Metal, 8 swing units, 8″ shelves (Fig. 63)	38.0	21	119.0	714	14,994	6,349	73.4
Ames, double range drawers with book supports (Fig. 64)	43.0	17	155.5	896	15,232	6,587	76.2*
Ames, double range drawers without book supports plus conventional shelves at end walls*	43.0	17+4.7 single-faced bracket sections	155.5 (drawer) 20.5 (bracket)	933 (drawer) 123.5 (bracket)	16,437	7,792	90.1
Hamilton drawers 18″ wide, 3′-10″ deep, 7 rows of shelves (Fig. 65)	46.0	58	52.1	312	18,096	9,451	109.3

*Storage capacity with Ames drawers could be increased to 933 volumes per unit if no book supports were used at the center of double-headed drawers. However, for orderly shelving, book supports were considered most desirable, entailing a loss of about 2.5 inches per double-headed drawer at the center. Without the employment of book supports, the number of volumes per bay would be 15,861, the gain over conventional shelving would be 7,216 or 83.7 per cent. In addition, if conventional wall shelving were placed along both end walls of the 6-bay area shown in Fig. 64 (leaving 6¼ inches clearance for one's hand when drawer is full open), the average number of volumes per bay would be further increased by 576 to a total of 16,437 volumes, representing a gain of 7,792 volumes over conventional shelving, or 90.1 per cent. However, Table 4 and Fig. 66 exclude this maximum capacity plan, involving a mixture of Ames and conventional units, so that comparisons can be limited to pure types in a continuous arrangement.

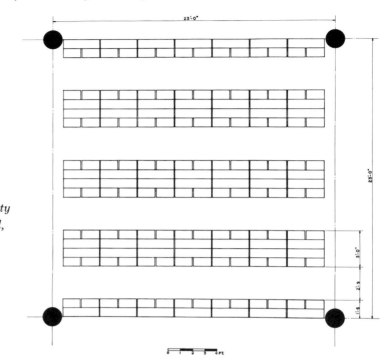

Fig. 62

Maximum capacity layout, Art Metal, 4 swing units.

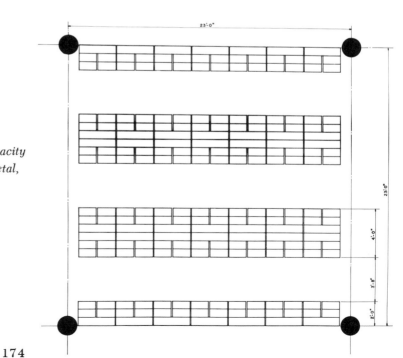

Fig. 63

Maximum capacity layout, Art Metal, 8 swing units.

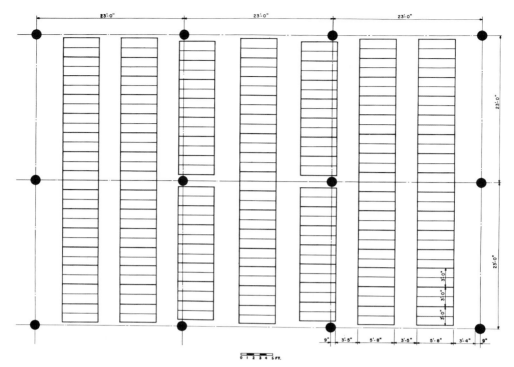

Fig. 64   *Maximum capacity layout, Ames.*

the Ames equipment layout covered 6 bays; and the data for Ames in Table 3 represented averages. (4) The systems were not equally adaptable to the particular shape and size of the bay for which they were considered. The most adaptable units were the Hamilton drawers since they were available in different widths and different depths. However, the other manufacturers could probably produce units of other-than-standard dimensions in the event of quantity orders.

Achievable percentage gain in storage capacity is not the only factor to be considered in the choice of compact storage equipment. Even though the Hamilton drawers achieve the greatest storage gain, some would-be users may prefer the Art Metal 4-swing units because they may seem easier to operate; others may prefer conventional stacks with narrow aisles because they consider complete visibility and uniform accessibility of the backs of books to be of primary importance.

In comparing storage capacity, we assumed identical ceiling height limitations that would allow only 7 rows of shelves. It should be mentioned, however, that additional storage capacity can be gained where ceilings are higher and where base footings

175

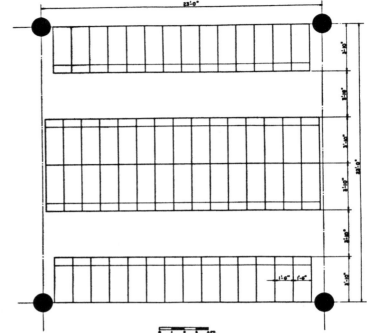

Fig. 65

*Maximum capacity
layout, Hamilton.*

and/or floors are strong enough to support additional loads. An installation in the basement floor of the new library building of the University of Wisconsin consists of 12 rows of drawers (Hamilton); the cost of compact storage drawers per volume shelved is slightly lower in such installations than it would be with only 7 rows of shelves. However, the upper drawers can be reached only by means of a movable lightweight stairway similar to the stairways used in connection with large airplanes; and the use of such stairways may increase the labor cost for the collecting and shelving of books and may cause accidents.

Building Cost. Turning now to the third variable, the building cost, we must ask: At what point of building cost does it become economical to resort to compact storage equipment for little used materials? Table 4 is designed to show the combined cost of shelving plus the cost of the floor area required for the shelving for each type of compact storage. It is only when we consider the cost of shelving and the building cost together that we gain a clear picture of the real cost of book storage. Compactness really means saving in building cost; and only if the saving in building cost is substantially greater than the cost of compact storage equipment will librarians resort to compact storage.

176

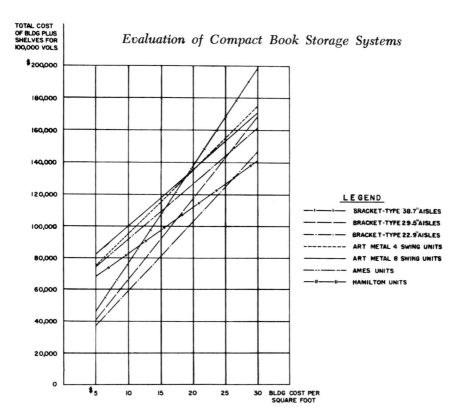

TOTAL COST
OF BLDG PLUS
SHELVES FOR
100,000 VOLS

LEGEND

—ı—ı— BRACKET-TYPE 38.7"AISLES
— — — BRACKET-TYPE 29.5"AISLES
—·—·— BRACKET-TYPE 22.9"AISLES
--------- ART METAL 4 SWING UNITS
——— ART METAL 8 SWING UNITS
—··—··— AMES UNITS
—ıı——ıı— HAMILTON UNITS

Fig. 66   *Total building cost plus shelving cost in relation to building cost per sq. ft. for 100,000 volumes. Comparison of different types of shelving.*

Current library building costs in the United States are high. It is doubtful whether air-conditioned buildings can be constructed at less than $13.00 per square foot in 1954. The air-conditioned library buildings of Oklahoma A & M College[12] and Georgia Institute of Technology[13] completed in 1953, cost about $20.00 per square foot without equipment; and some buildings currently under construction may cost as much as $25.00 per square foot. At such high cost levels, it may seem to become increasingly economical to use compact storage equipment for little-used materials that must be kept in the main library building.

12. Edmon Low, "Planned for Subject Areas," *Library Journal,* 78: 2189 (Dec. 15, 1953).
13. University of Georgia. *The Dedication of the Ilah Dunlap Little Library* (Athens, Ga., Nov. 19, 1953), p. 9.

Table 4

*Combined Cost of Shelving Plus Building Construction
for 100,000 Volumes at 6 Volumes per Linear Foot*

Type of Shelving	For Building Cost per Square Foot of				
	$5	$10	$15	$20	$25
Bracket-type shelving, 35.5″ aisles	15,300	15,300	15,300	15,300	15,300
Floor Area: 6119 square feet	30,595	61,190	91,785	122,380	152,975
Total	45,895	76,490	107,085	137,680	168,275
Bracket-type shelving, 30.7″ aisles	15,300	15,300	15,300	15,300	15,300
Floor Area: 5099 square feet	25,495	50,990	76,485	101,980	127,980
Total	40,795	66,290	91,785	117,280	143,280
Bracket-type shelving, 20.7″ aisles	15,300	15,300	15,300	15,300	15,300
Floor Area: 4371 square feet	21,855	43,710	65,565	87,420	109,275
Total	37,155	59,010	80,865	102,720	124,575
Art Metal, with 4 swing units	55,000	55,000	55,000	55,000	55,000
Floor Area: 4003 square feet	20,015	40,030	60,045	80,060	100,075
Total	75,015	95,030	115,045	135,060	155,075
Art Metal, with 8 swing units	64,706	64.706	64,706	64,706	64,706
Floor Area: 3535 square feet	17,675	35,350	53,025	70,700	88,375
Total	82,281	100,056	117,731	135,406	153,081
Ames units	57,000	57,000	57,000	57,000	57,000
Floor Area: 3473 square feet	17,365	34,730	52,085	69,460	86,825
Total	74,365	91,730	109,085	126,460	143,825
Hamilton units	53,667	53,667	53,667	53,667	53,667
Floor Area: 2923 square feet	14,615	29,230	43,845	58,360	73,075
Total	68,282	82,897	97,512	112,127	126,742

However, if the materials under question need not be kept in the main building, the total storage cost for such materials can be sizably reduced through the construction of a warehouse type building and the use of conventional bracket-type shelving. A warehouse building of the quonset type was constructed at Southern Illinois University in 1952/53 for $3.30 per square foot, exclusive of the cost of land and with no pro-rating for heating supplied from a central heating plant.

Table 5

*Costs of Conventional and Hamilton Shelving
for 100,000 Volumes in a Warehouse
Compared with the Same Shelving in a Library Building*

(A)	Bracket-type shelving Warehouse cost	$ 15,300		(C)	Hamilton drawers Warehouse cost	$ 53,667
	6119 sq. ft. @ $3.30	$ 20,193			2923 sq. ft. @ $3.30	$ 9,646
	Total	$ 35,493			Total	$ 63,313
(B)	Bracket-type shelving Library bldg. cost	$ 15,300		(D)	Hamilton drawers Library bldg. cost	$ 53,667
	6119 sq. ft. @ $20	$122,380			2923 sq. ft. @ $20	$ 58,460
	Total	$137,680			Total	$112,127

Saving in cost: Total A is 74.4% less than Total B.
Total C is 43.6% less than Total D.

According to Table 5, if your main building had a construction or replacement cost of $20 per square foot, the cheapest warehouse type of storage can cut the total cost of storing little-used materials by about 74.4 per cent as compared to conventional shelving (B compared to A), whereas savings obtainable through the most condensing compact storage equipment constitute only 18.5 per cent (B compared to D). Compact storage in a warehouse type building is 78.4 per cent more expensive than bracket-type shelving (C compared to A). Such shelving is luxury equipment appropriate for luxurious surroundings.

Before storage equipment is purchased, the crucial question to be answered is whether the materials need to be housed in the main building or not. Only if they must be housed in the main building should compact storage equipment be considered.

There is some question, however, as to whether a plain quonset type building is suitable for the storing of little-used library books over extended periods of time. Observations at a storage library in New England indicate that even little-used books should be protected from chemically damaging dust deposits, excessive air dryness, humidity, and heat. It was for these reasons that the Midwest Inter-Library Center in Chicago was equipped with complete air-conditioning, including refrigeration and de-humidification. Installation of such equipment raises, of course, the cost of building construction because it requires not only the purchase of expensive equipment but also more adequate thermal insulation and numerous ducts. In the case of an air-conditioned storage library currently being planned on a middle western campus, the cost per square foot without shelving equipment was estimated to be five to six times the figure assumed for a quonset type building. For such a building, compact storage equipment might be recommended.

Figure 66, which graphically portrays the data of Table 4, shows that, if these compact storage systems are compared with conventional stacks normally spaced, free-standing compact storage equipment begins to become economical only when the building cost per square foot amounts to about $12.00 in the case of Hamilton drawers, $16.00 in the case of Ames drawers, $19.00 in the case of Art Metal swing units. Moreover, if compact storage equipment is compared with the severe aisle reduction plan (22.9-inch aisles for 8-inch shelves), the most compressing type of compact stack does not begin to pay dividends until the building cost per square foot exceeds about $27.00. It must, therefore, be concluded that wherever there are no serious objections to the severe aisle reduction plan, it represents the least expensive type of compact book storage despite its inability to increase storage capacity by more than 40 per cent; and available compact storage equipment of the drawer and hinge types can bring about sizable additional economies only in fantastically expensive buildings or in situations where narrowed aisles between stack ranges are unacceptable.

The overall savings obtainable with the most condensing type of compact storage (Hamilton), as compared to regularly spaced conventional stacks, for the typical range of current building costs are shown in Table 6. (For raw data, see Table 4).

Table 6

Savings Through Compact Storage in Relation to Overall Cost

Building Cost per sq. ft.	Savings in Overall Cost
$10	— 8.2% (no saving!)
15	+ 8.9%
20	+18.6%
25	+24.7%
30	+29.0%

The overall percentage savings tend to increase as the building cost goes up, but percentagewise the savings tend to increase at a diminishing rate. Since few buildings are likely to cost over $30 per square foot, savings are not likely to exceed 29%; and for the typical building, savings will be within a range of 10 to 25%.

The point at which compact storage equipment begins to pay dividends would be lower if the cost of land plus the pro-rated cost of a power plant and steam pipe connections or the cost of a separate heating installation had to be included in the building cost. Such might be the case in centrally located metropolitan public libraries or in urban universities; in situations of this sort, it might pay to resort to compact storage stacks. These percentages expressing comparisons of total costs show the real savings in contrast to the savings expressed in terms of increase in storage capacity alone. The reason for such small real savings is, of course, the high cost of compact storage equipment in relation to conventional bracket-type shelving, which was shown, in Table 1, to be three to four times as high.

The Effect of Cross Aisles. Our comparative calculations of possible savings obtainable through compact storage systems were based on the assumption that no cross aisles would be provided in the stacks. In an open-stack "modular" library building, cross aisles might, indeed, be unnecessary, provided that no solid block of stacks extended beyond two bays on the narrow side of such a block and assuming that a reading room was located adjacent to one of the broad sides. If a stack block were two bays deep and no cross aisles were provided, stack ranges would be at most 46 feet long in a building with bays measuring 23 by 23 feet. Such a length, although not ideal, might be considered tolerable. Keyes D. Metcalf reported that a range length of 51 ft. was found acceptable at Harvard University,[14] although anything beyond 30 ft. has generally been regarded as inefficient.

If we assumed that 3 ft. wide cross aisles were provided in each bay, thus having no stack range extend beyond 18 to 20 ft. without a break, how would our calculations of comparative building plus shelving costs be affected? The answer is that compact storage equipment would show up somewhat more favorably as compared to an arrangement without cross aisles. For instance, at a building cost of $20.00 per square foot, the savings for Hamilton Compo stacks would be 23.0% as compared

14. *ACRL Monographs,* No. 10, Fall, 1953, p. 12.

to only 18.6% for an arrangement without cross aisles. The point at which compact storage equipment would begin to achieve genuine savings would thus be lower, and the savings would be slightly higher throughout the range of building costs. The provision of stack stairways would further contribute to making compact storage equipment appear in a slightly more favorable light. It is possible that such additional savings would be judged sufficiently higher by some librarians to overcome their reluctance to substitute compact storage for conventional stack equipment.

Multitier Stacks. It has been claimed that compact storage stacks appear in the most unfavorable light if comparisons are limited to single tier stacks, and that the advantages of compact storage stacks are greater in the case of multitier installations. To test this contention, data for the following contemplated building program for a university library stack annex in 1954 were analyzed: Assume a plot area measuring 20 feet by 60 feet and compare the costs of (1) a 4-story building framework, cement floors, plus *conventional* bracket type stack, with (2) a 4-story building framework, cement floors, plus *compact* stacks (Hamilton).

(1) Assuming ranges 55 inches on centers, conventional shelving would provide 3,052 linear feet of shelving per tier, or 12,208 linear feet for the 4 floors of the building. At 6 volumes per linear foot, *73,248 volumes* could be accommodated.

(2) Assuming Hamilton Compo ranges 8 feet on centers, the drawers measuring 18 by 48 inches, with 48-inch wide aisles, would provide 6,384 linear feet of shelving per tier, or 25,536 linear feet for the 4 floors of the building. At 6 volumes per linear foot, *153,216 volumes* would be accommodated.

In estimating the cost of the building, it was assumed that each floor would measure 1,200 square feet and that the total building would contain 36,000 cubic feet (1,200 square feet times 30 feet, for 4 tiers each 7 feet 6 inches high). Taking advantage of the stack structure to support a flat lightweight roof, the building cost was estimated to be $45,000, excluding stacks and electrical work for the stacks, but including building framework, first floor reinforced concrete floor, three steel stack decks, single-run stack stair. The total cost of the building construction, plus shelving and asphalt tile in aisles only, was estimated as follows:

(1) For conventional shelving accommodating 73,248 volumes: $76,940, or $1.03 per volume.

(2) For Hamilton Compo stacks accommodating 153,216 volumes: $130,000, or $ .85 per volume.

The savings per volume shelved for Hamilton Compo stacks as compared to conventional stacks would, therefore, amount to 17.5%; this difference can also be expressed the other way around by saying that conventional shelving costs 21.2% more than Hamilton Compo shelving. Is it desirable to abandon conventional shelving methods for the sake of achieving a 21.2% saving in overall cost? It seems doubtful whether compact storage equipment will be selected on the basis of currently achievable cost saving alone. If there are other advantages, however, as has been claimed, we may be doubly justified in selecting compact storage equipment; but if there are few other advantages and possibly some disadvantages, many librarians may decide to wait until compact storage equipment comes down considerably in price.

Other Factors. The representative of one manufacturer of compact stacks claimed that "it is a basic mistake to be so concerned about the cost of stack equipment" and that efficiency and convenience are much more important factors than cost alone. In other words, even if the use of compact storage stacks yields overall savings that are generally not in excess of 20%, there are many other advantages connected with compact storage that should eventually lead to the abandonment of conventional shelving in favor of compact storage for all book shelving: "We sincerely feel," to quote from a letter dated February 9, 1954, "that our design will in the long run prove a most satisfactory usable stack for practically every type of stack usage." This is, indeed, a startling claim. Let us, therefore, enumerate these other advantages:

(1) Lighting installation and maintenance will be substantially reduced.

(2) Installation of floor covering and floor maintenance will be substantially reduced because of the reduction of aisle space.

(3) In closed-stack libraries, the cost of carrying books to the delivery desk and of shelving returned books will be greatly reduced because of the reduction in travel distance.

(4) Installation and maintenance of heating and ventilating equipment may be cut in half.

(5) Janitorial and renovation costs will be lessened. All these factors are basically also cost-reducing factors that should be added to the savings of stack equipment obtainable through the use of compact storage stacks. To determine the exact magnitude

of these additional savings during the life-time of a building deserves the careful attention of a professional cost accountant.

These savings in cost must be balanced against disadvantages allegedly associated with compact storage equipment: (1) Books are less directly accessible. (2) Movable parts may require maintenance. (3) Moving of drawers or hinged doors causes noise. (4) Shelving, shifting, and collecting of books require more time and motion and, therefore, involve greater labor costs. (5) Drawers and hinged doors may block aisles and become hazards, causing accidents. (6) Time may have to be expended in teaching library users who are not mechanically inclined how to operate drawers or hinged doors with safety. (7) Compact storage units are not too practical in open stacks.

Summary. This paper has been concerned with the economics of compact storage. It was shown that compact storage equipment is expensive per volume shelved as compared to conventional bracket-type shelving, but that prices for the products of different manufacturers were fairly close together. Since different types of compact storage systems differed greatly in their ability to increase the storage capacity of a given floor area, it was necessary to take the cost of the floor area into account in the evaluation of different types of compact storage equipment. If the combined cost of the needed floor area and the compact storage equipment was compared with the combined cost of the needed floor area and conventional bracket-type shelving, savings of perhaps not over 25% could be obtained through compact storage equipment. For little-used materials, the least expensive method of compact storage would currently be the construction of an inexpensive storage warehouse where land and central heat are cheaply available. Further savings could, of course, be obtained through simple aisle reduction wherever free-standing ranges are used, through sizing, and through the shelving of books with their short edges presented to the aisles, as advocated and outlined by Fremont Rider for hinged and rolling stacks as well as conventional stacks.[15] Fremont Rider, in discussing compact storage equipment, before it became widely available and before drawer shelves had been discussed, was not very far off in his prediction that "the only place where savings would be effected would be in the amount (per book stored) of the stack building shell which would be

15. Rider, *op. cit.*, p. 61.

required; and though this saving might be material, the extra cost of the stack installation in it would probably more than offset the saving. What we have here again, in other words, is a greater compactness, but no over-all economy."[16] We should modify this statement by adding that under certain conditions some overall economy can now be achieved, but that the savings will not be very great and will probably not outweigh the disadvantage of semi-obstructed access to books in many situations where building expansion, aisle reduction, or conventional warehouse storage is possible.

The most profitable application of compact storage stacks may well be in the conversion of an existing conventional stack into a compact storage stack if existing stack columns can be utilized without the use of too much labor and if base footings are strong enough. Such conversion is apparently possible by means of the four-way columns developed by Remington Rand as well as by the Hamilton and Ames drawers; the Art Metal swing units can be used only where fixed stack aisles are wide enough to permit the installation of one or two additional shelf sections in each aisle or where stack ranges are free-standing. Conversion may be difficult, if not impossible, in cases where the dimensions of the old installation do not fit the dimensions of the particular compact storage equipment that has been selected. In all cases, a careful cost analysis is called for to determine actual as against impressionistic savings.

16. *Ibid.*, p. 34.

The text paper used in this book is "Permalife," a stable and enduring paper developed under a grant from the Council on Library Resources, Inc., and produced by the Standard Paper Manufacturing Company, Richmond, Virginia.